THE FIRST YEAR

AT

PLYMOUTH PLANTATION

MOURT'S RELATION

A JOURNAL OF THE PILGRIMS AT PLYMOUTH

A RELATION OR JOURNAL OF THE ENGLISH PLANTATION SETTLED AT PLYMOUTH IN NEW ENGLAND, BY CERTAIN ENGLISH ADVENTURERS BOTH MERCHANTS AND OTHERS.

1622

Knowledge Keepers Editon, 2022

ISBN: 978-1-7377062-8-1

CONTENTS

Preface

This edition of Mourt's Relation was edited by Dwight B. Heath, and published in 1963. Mr. Heath made valuable contributions in his "Editor's Introduction" and "Notes on this Edition," as well as in numerous footnotes.

60 years later, America has devolved into a less-educated populace, preferring short bits of text online to old historic documents. What you hold in your hands is a treasure trove of exciting adventure coupled with facts that have lately been misrepresented.

While William Bradford's personal narrative of the Plymouth Colony (Of Plymouth Plantation) presents us with a detailed history of the Pilgrims, this little book is the short version. Mourt's Relation is the epitome of primary American history sources, and is exactly why Knowledge Keepers exists.

No matter what kind of history is presented in 21st century America, the words written down by the men and women who lived it, observed it, and knew it are still the truth upon which we can depend.

In this Knowledge Keepers edition of Mourt's Relation, I have added chapter headings to each important section, where you will find a bit more explanation of the people and the times, for those who are new to the actual Pilgrims' story. There are additional footnotes to clarify the meaning of outdated words (differentiated from the 1963 footnotes of Mr. Heath with *italics*), as well as illustrations for fun and for education.

As Americans fall prey to confusion surrounding the truth about the Pilgrims, about Puritans, their intent, and their relationship with the Indians, you can own the truth in a simple, printed form. As I tell my children and my history students, the internet is not your friend when it comes to historic fact. But the old texts are still alive, and whether we like what happened or not, at least we can know the truth.

I hope you enjoy this and share it with your children and grandchildren. Pass on the truth, and keep it alive.

Nicki Truesdell

Founder, Knowledge Keepers Bookstore

November 2022

EDITOR'S INTRODUCTION

By Dwight B. Heath, 1963

Background

The coming of the Pilgrims and their establishment of the Plymouth Plantation is one of the great adventures in the American experience. This book is the earliest published account of that adventure, a day-by-day journal written in a simple forceful manner by men who took part in it. The story is familiar[1]— deceptively familiar, in that portions of it have undergone a complex process of transformation and emerge as modern myths in our national folklore. Still it is a story full of glory, and of tragedy, which deserves a wider public.

The glory, as usual, exists mostly in retrospect. The Separatists had already shown the courage of their convictions in defying both Church and State by worshiping in their own way in England. They had

---

[1] An immense body of literature, both popular and scholarly, has been written on the story of the Pilgrims, and much of it is excellent. One of the most comprehensive accounts is also one of the most enjoyable; George F. Willison's *Saints and Strangers* (New York, 1945) combines exhaustive scholarship with style and wit.

3

finally been driven to take refuge in Holland, the only European nation where they could then enjoy complete religious tolerance. After twelve years of poverty and social isolation in Amsterdam and Leyden, the self-styled "Saints"[2] sought the New World largely as a land of economic opportunity where they hoped to start afresh. Similar motives undoubtedly moved the "Strangers,"[3] the motley group of fellow travelers who joined the party at Plymouth, England, and doubled their numbers. The "Strangers" were loyal to the Church of England, as were the few indentured servants and hired men, who soon comprised a dissident faction. They cared no more for freedom of conscience than did the "merchant adventurers," a joint stock company of about seventy London businessmen who sponsored the plantation only as a commercial venture likely to yield high profits.

Some have read the "Mayflower Compact" as the glorious cornerstone of American democracy, but it seems hardly revolutionary in context here where it first appeared in print. The fact that the Pilgrims enjoyed warm relations with some Indians is also much to their credit, but it may reflect the charity of the Indians at least as much as their own benevolence. Still one cannot belittle the achievement of these simple people. They consistently showed resourcefulness in coping with new problems, and

---

[2] In the Biblical sense of "God's chosen people," or simply, "members of a Christian church."

[3] So-called because they were unknown to members of the Leyden congregation, having been enlisted by the sponsors of the expedition.

courage in the face of danger. The greatest glory of the Pilgrims may well have been the ardent faith and dogged persistence which saw them through great tragedy.

Although there is little talk of tragedy in this volume, we know that more than half of the original party died during the first year at Plymouth.[4] Considering their primitive living conditions, it is a wonder that so many did survive the "general sickness" while wading to and from the shallop, and working hard to develop new skills in the harsh and alien environment of a strenuous New England winter. Another tragedy is only presaged here, in the white man's facile rationalization of his usurpation of lands which had long been used by Indians. Within the span of a single lifetime, the indigenous peoples were dispossessed, and their way of life did not long survive after the mutually debilitating "King Philip's War." The tragedy and the glory of Pilgrims and Indians alike emerge in a careful reading of this journal.

About the Book

Any good book must mean many things to many readers, and this journal offers more than just reflections of past glories and intimations of great tragedy. It is a primary source for American history in that critical period when a beach-head of Anglo culture was established in the New World. In this volume are

---

[4] *Much of this is found in William Bradford's book, Of Plymouth Plantation.*

the earliest accounts of the "Mayflower Compact," the establishment of a community which has become focal in our national heritage, the signing of this country's first mutual security pact, and the famous first Thanksgiving. There is no question of the book's essential authenticity, and most of it has the flavor of having been written on the spot at the time.

This sense of immediacy also enhances the value of the journal as a well written story of true adventure. The protagonists quietly suppressed an impending mutiny, even before they landed. While exploring the unknown wastes of Cape Cod, they conducted archeological excavations before they had a roof over their heads. They were attacked by Indians, and yet persisted, built their homes in a foreign land, and soon traveled freely among the natives. This is high adventure indeed!

Political implications are of some importance too. The passengers on the *Mayflower* are famous for their founding of "a civil body politic ... to enact, constitute, and frame such just and equal laws, ordinances, acts, [and] offices from time to time, as shall be thought most meet and convenient for the general good of the colony." Within less than a week of their first conversation with an Indian, the Pilgrims signed an enduring peace treaty with Massasoit, a leader of the neighboring Wampanoags. A year later, they enjoyed trading relations and military alliance with many other Indian groups.

The journal may also be viewed as a valuable ethnographic document. Although previous sporadic contacts by explorers and traders had yielded some impressionistic descriptions[5], the Pilgrims were the first Europeans to be in close and sustained contact with the Indians of southern New England. At first they expected only hostility from the "savages," but it was not long before they found valuable helpers in Squanto and Samoset, both of whom had learned already some English when they were kidnapped and sold as slaves by English traders. The Pilgrims were obliged to work out a modus vivendi with these "tall and proper men" whose dress seemed outlandish, whose foods were strange, and whose customs were curious enough to deserve description. We are indebted to the authors of this journal for a wealth of information about such patterns during the brief period before they disappeared forever. There are many aspects of the native ways of life of which the Pilgrims were unaware, and others which they treated with only tantalizing brevity, but a wealth of irreplaceable ethnographic data in this volume serves to illuminate our fragmentary understanding of coastal Algonquian cultures.

Just as we can learn much about the Indians from this book, we can also gain rich insights into the character of the Pilgrims themselves. Mention of the threat of mutiny explodes the hoary myth of dedicated unity of purpose among all members of the party. The bravery

---

[5] *See the Knowledge Keepers book, "Valiant Navigators" for the journals of these explorers.*

of the Pilgrims emerges in bold relief, as does their readiness to rob the graves of Indians. In light of this text, their industriousness cannot be doubted. Flashes of humor occur, and their strong sense of being a "chosen people" is clearly manifest in recurrent references to a felicitous "divine providence."

"Human interest" is not lacking either. We can imagine the chagrin of William Bradford unwittingly caught up in a deer snare, just as we can sympathize with the consternation created when a prankish boy fired his father's musket in a ship's cabin where open kegs of gunpowder lay about. It is easy to feel for the "old [Indian] woman whom we judged to be no less than a hundred years old" who wept because "she was deprived of the comfort of her children in her old age" when Capt. Hunt kidnapped her three sons. And how his playmates must have envied the boy who was lost on Cape Cod, and was returned by the Nauset Indians, "behung with beads"!

Within this brief but diverse book there is also a pervasive mystery, for no one knows who wrote it. The book has become known as *Mourt's Relation*, but it is not the unitary effort of a single man. Five of the ten "chapters" have bylines, and Mourt's contribution is almost the briefest of the ten. The mystery deepens when we confess not knowing much about the man named Mourt. Perhaps the most fruitful way to approach the problem is through a discussion of the several components of the book.

It opens with a dedicatory letter of transmittal "To his much respected friend...." This is a form of profuse and discursive acknowledgment typical of the time. It seems to have been appended by an associate of the settlers, whose concern was "... but the recommendation of the relation itself," to a distinguished member of the "merchant adventurers" who had sponsored the *Mayflower* voyage. The dedication is signed *R.G.*, which I assume to be a misprint for the initials of Robert Cushman. The only member of the party at Plymouth with initials R.G. was Richard Gardiner, an undistinguished "Stranger" who stayed only briefly and took little part in the venture. The fact that misprints are frequent throughout the rest of the book suggests the possibility of reference to Cushman, who is a person most likely to have drafted such a letter. As a deacon of the Leyden congregation who also served as their business agent, he was instrumental in securing English permission for removal to the New World, and, after having had to turn back on the unseaworthy *Speedwell*, he continued negotiations with the "merchant adventurers" while the *Mayflower* sailed on to Plymouth. Visiting the plantation on the second ship, *Fortune*, he delivered the patent which confirmed their legal right to settle there, together with a stringent contract from the sponsors, which he finally induced the Pilgrims to sign, after preaching a pointed sermon on "The Dangers of Self-Love[i]." The manuscript of the relations must have been carried back to England with him on the *Fortune* in December of 1621.

9

Appended at the end of the volume is another chapter which I attribute to Cushman. A long exposition of "Reasons and considerations touching the lawfulness of removing out of England into the parts of America," signed *R.C.*, is a thinly veiled promotional tract organized like a sermon, which cites Scripture to justify the plantation and to persuade others to follow.

Among the prefatory letters is one containing "Certain useful advertisements ..." and signed *I.R.*. We are told that this letter of advice concerning man's proper relation with God and with his fellow men was "... written by a discreet friend unto the planters in New England, at their first setting sail from Southampton."[6] This "unfeigned well-willer" is most likely John Robinson, pastor of the expatriate Separatist congregation in Leyden, and hence understandably solicitous for the welfare of the Pilgrims, and also in a position to proffer such counsel. The letter may have been appended to this book especially to serve as a model of morality for those "Strangers" who might hopefully be induced to emigrate and join the party at Plymouth.

---

[6] The Pilgrims originally embarked in two ships at Southampton, 5 August 1620, but because the *Speedwell* leaked dangerously they put in at Dartmouth for repairs. When they returned to the open sea, they discovered that she still shipped water. Turning to the nearest port, they reluctantly decided to abandon the *Speedwell* as unseaworthy, and many of the party transferred to the already crowded *Mayflower*, while a few decided to defer their emigration. The successful voyage from Plymouth began 6 September, with their third departure from the homeland.

Five "relations" constitute the major portion of the book, and none of these is signed. The first and longest, on "The proceedings of the plantation ...," begins with the departure from Plymouth, England, and recounts events of the next six months, including the voyage, the signing of the "compact," the several "discoveries," the choice of a site and the building there, as well as early contacts with the Indians, culminating in the signing of a peace treaty with Massasoit. A second deals with "A journey to Pokanoket ..." and describes further friendly dealings with the Wampanoag Indians. The next treats "A voyage ... to the Kingdom of Nauset, to seek a boy that had lost himself in the woods...." An account of "A journey to Nemasket ..." shows how the Pilgrims sought to defend their Indian allies against the hostile Narragansets, and "A relation of our voyage to the Massachusetts ..." describes the expansion of trade relations to the north.

According to the dedicatory letter, these vivid reports were "... writ by the several actors themselves, after their plain and rude manner." It is almost certain that the principal author was Edward Winslow, although it is generally believed that William Bradford also had a hand in the effort. Both of these men were among the few who were prominent in the affairs of the plantation, and they two are the only ones of the first party who obviously enjoyed writing. Winslow's *Good News from New England* (London, 1624), continued the narrative of the plantation from the time when this volume left off, and is markedly similar in style.

In his *Good News ...*, Winslow mentions descriptions of aspects of Indian culture which were prepared by "... myself and others, in former letters, (which came to the press against my will and knowledge) ..."; I know of no publication other than *Mourt's Relation* to which this could refer. Bradford's manuscript history *Of Plymouth Plantation* (first published in Boston, 1856) has become the principal source on the Pilgrim experience, although he could hardly be said to claim priority when he "... first began these scribbled writings (which was about the year 1630 and so pieced up at times of leisure afterward)." His treatment of the first year at Plymouth is a curious combination, consisting largely of passages identical with those in *Mourt's Relation*, together with discursive classical allusions and philosophic ruminations. Bradford's style generally tends to be more analytic than descriptive, and the specificity of detail which makes this text such a rich source material for the historian and ethnographer rarely occurs elsewhere in Bradford's work. It is entirely within the realm of possibility that he may have incorporated in his manuscript the work of others as it had appeared in *Mourt's Relation*; he freely adopted material from other sources.

The ensuing "Letter sent from New England ... setting forth ... the worth of that plantation ...," follows the five narrative relations closely in style, and is signed by *E.W.* It is almost certainly Winslow who here sounds vaguely like a twentieth-century Florida real estate agent when he describes the first Thanksgiving as indicating the richness of the land: "I never in my life remember a more seasonable year than we have here enjoyed and if we have once but kine[7], horses, and sheep, I make no question but men might live as contented here as in any part of the world." He also includes some very specific suggestions concerning the practical needs of those who might choose to come.

And what was Mourt's contribution to the book which has been linked with his name by historians, librarians, and bibliographers since Prince[8] first invented the convenient title, *Mourt's Relation*, as a substitute for the cumbersome original? A brief foreword, or introduction, "To the reader," is all that we must credit to the signer, one *G. Mourt*. It may have been he who was responsible for bringing to press this collection of papers, "... hoping of a cheerful proceeding, both of adventurers and planters." He explicitly denied authorship of the narratives: "These relations coming to my hand from my both known and faithful friends, on whose writings I do much rely, I thought it not amiss to make them more general...." But scholars still do not know who he was!

It is suggested that he had at some time been associated with the authors of the relations, whom he called "my both known and faithful friends." It is also suggested that he had long hoped to emigrate to the New World, "... as myself then much desired, and

---

[7] *cattle*
[8] Thomas Prince, *A Chronological History of New England ...* (Boston, 1736), vol. I, pt. 2, p. 71, fn. 38.

13

shortly hope to effect, if the Lord will, the putting to of my shoulder in this hopeful business." These criteria clearly apply to Robert Cushman, who, as we have seen, was a person who might appropriately have introduced such a book.

The specifications also apply to another member of the Leyden congregation who was active in negotiating with the "merchant adventurers" until he did sail to Plymouth, on the first ship bound for the plantation after the book was printed. If no more than the initials had been given in the signature to the introduction— as was the case in every other portion of the volume— there would be little hesitation to identify the author as George Morton.

As it is, however, one must attempt to account for the discrepancy in name if he suggests that it may have been Morton who wrote it. It is easy to suggest that the use of "Mourt" for "Morton" could have been merely another of the many misprints in the book. At least as plausible, however, is the suggestion that it may have been a pseudonym. It is not difficult to imagine why there might have been some attempt to conceal the fact *if* Morton had been intimately involved in the preparation and promulgation of the book. A printer might have been reluctant to "publish" a document written by Separatists unless it carried an introduction by an apparently disinterested party. In a period of strict royal control of the press in England, William Brewster of the Leyden congregation had already incurred the wrath of King James by printing an outspoken opposition tract, *Perth Assembly* (Leyden, 1619), so that any writings by his friends and associates might logically also be suspect. Furthermore, the fact that *Mourt's Relation* is essentially a promotional effort is clearly implied in the phrasing of the original title, describing the "safe arrival" of the "English planters," and "their joyful building of, and comfortable planting themselves in the now well defended town of New Plymouth." In such an effort to excite more prospective settlers, it would have been sound public relations to minimize the degree of identification between the plantation and the "Saints," who were popularly scorned as heretics and criminals.

Another possibility must be mentioned. I am only half-joking when I suggest that at least this portion of *Mourt's Relation* may actually have been written by someone named G. Mourt, of whom we know nothing else. One of the delights of historical research is the fact that one always raises more questions than he can answer. The mystery remains.

Mourt's Relation is clearly a book which offers different meanings to every reader. I hope that this edition may reach a broad audience and increase popular understanding of a neglected portion of the American experience.

A Note on This Edition

My intention is to provide the contemporary reader with an appreciation of this exciting book as it was received by an eager and curious public when it was first published almost three and a half centuries ago. In keeping with this aim, the entire text is included here, in the order of the original.[9] So that the authors may speak forcefully and directly to the reader of today, I have introduced only uniform spelling, punctuation, and paragraphing, structural niceties which were of no concern to authors or printers until late in the eighteenth century. The eloquent English language of the period is familiar to us all, through the King James version of the Bible or the works of Shakespeare, and I have scrupulously left each word intact. The text, then, is reproduced verbatim, including marginalia, chapter headings, and running heads, altered only by the use of modern orthography for the sake of clarity.

I have deliberately avoided distracting the reader from the original text, by introducing a minimum of footnotes. Some annotation seems indispensable for

---

[9] Although portions of the book have been reprinted frequently, the only other presentation of the full text was a facsimile in an edition limited to 285 copies, prepared by Henry M. Dexter, and entitled *Mourt's Relation* (Boston, 1865). It is a heavily annotated volume, and Dexter's monumental effort has aided a generation of scholars, but his meticulous attention to "faithful reproduction of the original, letter for letter" makes it formidable to any but a dedicated student. The best known and most widely available edition includes annotation and uniform spelling, but is marred by some minor omissions and transpositions: Alexander Young, *Chronicles of the Pilgrim Fathers* (Boston, 1841), pp. 110-249.

understanding the work of another age, but this edition does not bear the tender burden of scholarly disquisition. Modern equivalents are given for archaic words and place-names, and I have offered brief explanations of a few outdated allusions. Dates are retained as in the original, so that ten days must be added to any date given in the text in order to fit it into the modern Gregorian calendar, which was not adopted by England and her colonies until 1752.

In the exacting task of collating this text with the original, I was helped by my friend and colleague, Anna Mae Cooper. We worked in the John Carter Brown Library where Thomas R. Adams kindly put excellent facilities at our disposal, including the library's copy of the first edition of the book, as well as the Smith and Champlain maps. Lucille Hanna first introduced me to the excitement of history, and J. L. Giddings pointed out the ethnographic value of *Mourt's Relation*. Miss Rose T. Briggs, Director of Pilgrim Hall, shared her enthusiasm and broad knowledge of the Pilgrims. E. Lawrence Couter, David Freeman, Arthur G. Pyle, Muriel Stefani, and the entire staff of Plimoth Plantation were helpful in many ways, and the corporation generously provided the photographs. The title page, ornamental letters and top-page designs are reproduced from a copy of the original, now in possession of the Rhode Island Historical Society. Mrs. N. Mac Donald typed from a difficult manuscript.

An adventure such as this rightfully belongs to all who would chase rainbows!

DWIGHT B. HEATH
Brown University
Providence, R. I.

SAMUEL DE CHAMPLAIN'S MAP OF PLYMOUTH HARBOR

Although the Pilgrims were the first Europeans to establish a permanent colony in northeastern North America, they did not come to an unknown land. As early as 1605, Samuel de Champlain had mapped Plymouth Harbor[10], in the course of a three-year expedition during which he explored the coast from Nova Scotia to Martha's Vineyard. The quality of his detailed and accurate observations on the land and people appears in this map, and in his notes on the visit: "There came to us two or three canoes, which had just been fishing for cod and other fish which are found there in large numbers. These they catch with hooks made of a piece of wood, to which they attach a bone in the shape of a spear and fasten it very securely. The whole has a fang-shape, and the line attached to it is made out of the bark of a tree. They gave me one of their hooks, which I took out of curiosity. In it the bone was fastened on by hemp, like that in France, as it seemed to me, and they told me that they gathered this plant without being obliged to cultivate it, and indicated that it grew to the height of four or five feet. This canoe went back on shore to give notice to their fellow inhabitants, who caused columns of smoke to arise on our account. We saw eighteen or twenty savages, who came to the shore and began to

---

[10] *Valiant Navigators: Sailors' Narratives of Voyages Along the New England Coast 1524-1624; Knowledge Keepers Bookstore, 2022, p. 67.*

dance. Our canoe landed in order to give them some bagatelles, at which they were greatly pleased. Some of them came to us and begged us to go to their river. We weighed anchor to do so, but were unable to enter on account of the small amount of water, it being low tide, and were accordingly obliged to anchor at the mouth. I went ashore, where I saw many others, who received us very cordially. I made also an examination of the river, but saw only an arm of water extending a short distance inland, where the land is only in part cleared. Running into this is merely a brook not deep enough for boats except at full tide. The circuit of the bay is about a league. On one side of the entrance to this bay there is a point which is almost an island, covered with wood, principally pines, and adjoins sandbanks, which are very extensive. On the other side, the land is high. There are two islets in this bay, which are not seen until one has entered, and around which it is almost entirely dry at low tide. This place is very conspicuous from the sea, for the coast is very low, excepting the cape at the entrance to the bay. We named it the Port du Cap. St. Louis...".

Reproduced is a copy from a first edition of *Les Voyages du Sieur de Champlain* (Paris, 1613), now in possession of the John Carter Brown Library.

CAPTAIN JOHN SMITH'S MAP OF NEW ENGLAND

The Pilgrims were familiar with Capt. John Smith's account of a voyage in which he had surveyed the coast from Cape Cod to Penobscot Bay in 1614.[11] He had even offered his services as guide and military captain, but Myles Standish got the job.[12] Undoubtedly they did bring with them his *Description of New England* (London, 1616), in which the following map was published.

Capt. Smith, who had already gained some fame and fortune in Virginia, dedicated to Prince Charles this effort in which the term "New England" first appeared: "... it being my chance to range some other parts of America, whereof I here present your highness the description in a map, my humble suit [in original, "sure"] is you would please to change their barbarous names for such English, as posterity may say Prince Charles was their godfather." Several English place-names were incorporated in the map, but posterity disregarded most of them, a noteworthy exception being "Plimouth." Smith notes that the Indians called the site "... Accomack, an excellent good harbor, good land, and no want of any thing but industrious people," recalling that "After much kindness, upon a small occasion we fought also with 40 or 50 of those

---

[11] *Valiant Navigators: Sailors' Narratives of Voyages Along the New England Coast 1524-1624; Knowledge Keepers Bookstore, 2022, p. 183.*.
[12] *Miles Standish, Puritan Captain; Knowledge Keepers Bookstore, 2021.*

[Indians]; though some were hurt and some slain, yet within an hour after, they became friends."

The map was subsequently reissued in several other works by Smith, additions being made on the engraved copper plate from time to time, to indicate more recent discoveries and settlements.

The copy reproduced here is from a first edition, now in possession of the John Carter Brown Library; obviously the representations of European-style buildings were as inappropriate as were the illustrations of monsters, introduced by imaginatively artistic cartographers. (The note concerning Smith's death was written in ink by a previous owner of this copy.)

24

A
RELATION OR

Iournall of the beginning and proceedings
of the Englifh Plantation fetled at *Plimoth* in N E W
E N G L A N D, by certaine Englifh Aduenturers both
Merchants and others.

With their difficult paffage, their fafe ariuall, their
ioyfull building of, and comfortable planting them-
felues in the now well defended Towne
of N E W P L I M O T H.

AS ALSO A RELATION OF FOVRE
feuerall difcoueries fince made by fome of the
fame Englifh Planters there refident.

I. In a iourney to P V C K A N O K I C K *the habitation of the Indians greateft King* Maffafoyt : *as alfo their meffage, the anfwer and entertainment
they had of him.*

I I. In a voyage made by ten of them to the Kingdome of Nawfet, *to feeke
a boy that had loft himfelfe in the woods : with fuch accidents as befell them
in that voyage.*

I I I. In their iourney to the Kingdome of Namafcnet, *in defence of their
greateft King* Maffafoyt, *againft the* Narrohigganfets, *and to reuenge the
fuppofed death of their Interpreter* Tifquantum.

I I I I. Their voyage to the Maffachufets, *and their entertainment there.*

With an anfwer to all fuch obiections as are any way made
againft the lawfulneffe of Englifh plantations
in thofe parts.

LONDON,
Printed for *Iohn Bellamie,* and are to be fold at his fhop at the two
Greyhounds in Cornhill neere the Royall Exchange, 1622.

Chapter 1: Prelude to Plymouth – and the United States of America

The Pilgrims, as we know them today, were not a band of explorers and adventures, set on making their fortune in the new world. Though other colonies were specifically begun for that reason, this little colony had very different needs and desires from the very beginning. They were Puritans, English Christians who had separated themselves from the Church of England on principle.

To understand them, we must go further back in history, to the invention of the printing press. Johann Gutenberg's 15th century marvel changed the world almost overnight (at least, in a Medieval sense.) Information finally had the ability to be spread in multiple languages and numerous copies. But it wasn't just the spread of information that was so widespread; the Holy Bible in print was about to change the world.

Gutenberg's first book was a copy of the Latin Bible. Numerous copies were made and distributed widely. In 1522, Martin Luther translated the Latin New Testament (and in 1534 the complete Bible) into German so his fellow Germans could read it for themselves. In 1526, William Tyndale translated the New Testament into the English language.
During these decades of biblical translation, the Protestant Reformation was reaching its height. It was this event that shook the religious world, and took

worldwide power away from the Roman Catholic Church.

Until this point in time, the scriptures and the church services were in Latin only, though not everyone was educated in Latin. What this meant was that a large percentage of Christendom was taught what to believe and how to be saved by the Church in Rome, who was adding new rules and requirements that were not scriptural. As more common people became familiar with the text of the scriptures, the fire of reformation spread.

What does any of this have to do with the Plymouth colony?

Now we come to the time of King Henry VIII of England. You may already be familiar with the story of his infatuation with Anne Boleyn, his Queen's lady-in-waiting. Henry wanted to divorce his first wife Catherine, but the Pope refused to grant his request. Tired of waiting for permission, Henry used the Protestant Reformation to his advantage.

The English Parliament passed the Acts of Supremacy in 1534, breaking from the Catholic Church and creating the Church of England, with Henry as Supreme Head of the Church of England. He promptly divorced Catherine and married Anne.

Now England was no longer Catholic (though Henry's daughter Mary would try to reinstate Catholicism during her brief reign). However, the Church of England was still very similar to the Roman Catholic Church in many ways. And thus began the rise of the Puritans.

The Puritan movement was once in which English Christians began to speak out against the practices of the Church of England, proclaiming the similar issues Luther had listed in his famed 95 theses. They objected to endless rules and regulations imposed by the church that were considered "human traditions" and not the plain truth of scriptures. There is far too much Puritan history to include here, but suffice it to say that Queen Elizabeth and her successor, King James, did work with the Puritan movement for the most part. But, the Anglican church under James became more tyrannical.

This led to a smaller sect of Puritans, called Separatists. Instead of trying to reform the Church of England from the inside, these Puritans decided the only true way to worship God was in their own churches, separate from the oversight of the official Church. They often met in secret to avoid arrest. Many of them were hounded, arrested, and abused for their actions.

So we find William Bradford's little group of Puritans leaving England (first settling in Holland for several years), and making the voyage to America to find freedom. Among the many colonies of New England in the 17ᵗʰ century, this is one of the most successful, peaceful, and influential in American history.

A relation or journal of the beginning and proceedings of the English Plantation settled at *Plymouth* in New England, by certain English adventurers both merchants and others. With their difficult passage, their safe arrival, their joyful building of, and comfortable planting themselves in the now well defended town of New Plymouth.

AS ALSO A RELATION OF FOUR
several discoveries since made by some of the same English Planters there resident.

I. *In a journey to* **Pokanoket**[13], *the habitation of the Indians' greatest King* **Massasoit**: *as also their message, the answer and entertainment they had of him.*

II. *In a voyage made by ten of them to the Kingdom of* **Nauset**, *to seek a boy that had lost himself in the wood: with such accidents as befell them in that voyage.*

III. *In their journey to the Kingdom of* **Nemasket**, *in defense of their greatest King* **Massasoit**, *against the* **Narragansets**, *and to revenge the supposed death of their Interpreter* **Squanto**.

---

[13] *The Pokanoket (also spelled Pakanokick) was the village governed by Massasoit (Wampanoag, c. 1581–1661). The term broadened to refer to all peoples and lands governed by Massasoit and his successors, which were part of the Wampanoag people in what is now Rhode Island and Massachusetts.*

IIII. *Their voyage to the* **Massachusetts**, *and their entertainment there.*

With an answer to all such objections as are any way made against the lawfulness of English plantations in those parts.

LONDON,
Printed for *John Bellamie*, and are to be sold at his shop at the Two Greyhounds in Cornhill near the Royal Exchange. 1622.

Chapter 2: Letter of Robert Cushman

Cushman was one the leaders of the Separatist movement before the Pilgrims sailed on the Mayflower.

Early on, he was involved in speaking out boldly against the Church of England and its "superstitious" practices. He was arrested for libel for producing handwritten notices and distributing them in Canterbury.

In 1611 he emigrated to Leiden, Holland, with a group of Puritans to escape the tyranny of the Church of England. They remained there for several years, but were dissatisfied. Around 1619, they began to make plans for a settlement in the American wilderness, with Robert Cushman as an agent for the Puritans in England.

Plans were made, and the Mayflower and Speedwell departed from Dartmouth in August of 1621, but the Speedwell had numerous problems and was forced to turn back. 120 passengers were forced to give up their plans and remain behind. Robert Cushman and his family were among this number.

Cushman did sail to Plymouth the following year with his son, but remained only a short time. On the return voyage he carried this Relation, to print and distribute.

Before his planned return to the Plymouth Colony, Robert Cushman died in Kent.

"As a deacon of the Leyden congregation who also served as their business agent, he was instrumental in securing English permission for removal to the New World, and, after having had to turn back on the unseaworthy *Speedwell*, he continued negotiations with the "merchant adventurers" while the *Mayflower* sailed on to Plymouth. Visiting the plantation on the second ship, *Fortune*, he delivered the patent which confirmed their legal right to settle there, together with a stringent contract from the sponsors, which he finally induced the Pilgrims to sign, after preaching a pointed sermon on "The Dangers of Self-Love." (See Endnotes for the complete sermon.) The manuscript of the relations must have been carried back to England with him on the *Fortune* in December of 1621." (See Introduction)

TO HIS MUCH
respected friend, Mr. I. P.[14]

Good Friend:

As we cannot but account it an extraordinary blessing
of God in directing our course for these parts, after we
came out of our native country, for that we had the
happiness to be possessed of the comforts we receive
by the benefit of one of the most pleasant, most
healthful, and most fruitful parts of the world; so must
we acknowledge the same blessing to be multiplied
upon our whole company, for that we obtained the
honor to receive allowance and approbation of our free
possession and enjoying thereof, under the authority of
those thrice honored persons, the President
and Council for the Affairs of New England, by whose
bounty and grace, in that behalf, all of us are tied to
dedicate our best service unto them,[15] as those under
his Majesty, that we owe it unto, whose noble
endeavors in these their actions the God of heaven and

---

[14] Presumably, the initials of John Peirce. Peirce was a London businessman one of the
"merchant adventurers" who had contributed to the *Mayflower's* first voyage. It is possible
that he underwrote the printing of the book; it is certain that the patent to lands occupied by
the Pilgrims—as virtual squatters for almost a year—was finally issued in his name, in trust
for the settlers. They were delighted to receive this confirmation of their legal rights, and
may have dedicated the book to him in gratitude. Only later did they learn of the many
devious ways in which he tried to cheat them.

[15] Acknowledging their indebtedness to Sir Ferdinando Gorges and his partners in the
Council for New England, (formerly, the Second Virginia Company, and the
Plymouth Company), who exercised legal authority over the area, which had
previously been called "Northern Virginia."

earth multiply to his glory and their own eternal comforts.

As for this poor relation, I pray you to accept it, as being writ by the several actors themselves, after their plain and rude manner; therefore doubt nothing of the truth thereof. If it be defective in any thing, it is their ignorance, that are better acquainted with planting than writing. If it satisfy those that are well affected to the business, it is all I care for. Sure I am the place we are in, and the hopes that are apparent, cannot but suffice any that will not desire more than enough. Neither is there want of aught among us but company to enjoy the blessings so plentifully bestowed upon the inhabitants that are here. While I was a-writing this, I had almost forgot that I had but the recommendation of the relation itself to your further consideration, and therefore I will end without saying more, save that I shall always rest

Yours in the way of friendship,

R. G.[16] From Plymouth, in New England.

---

[16] Presumably a misprint for the initials of Robert Cushman. See Introduction.

Chapter 3: Mourt's actual letter

This book has been known as "Mourt's Relation" throughout history, which is odd, since it was written by Edward Winslow and William Bradford.

As editor Dwight B. Heath says,

". . .what was Mourt's contribution to the book which has been linked with his name by historians, librarians, and bibliographers since Prince[17] first invented the convenient title, *Mourt's Relation*, as a substitute for the cumbersome original? A brief foreword, or introduction, "To the reader," is all that we must credit to the signer, one *G. Mourt*. It may have been he who was responsible for bringing to press this collection of papers, "... hoping of a cheerful proceeding, both of adventurers and planters." He explicitly denied authorship of the narratives: "These relations coming to my hand from my both known and faithful friends, on whose writings I do much rely, I thought it not amiss to make them more general...." But scholars still do not know who he was!

It is suggested that he had at some time been associated with the authors of the relations, whom he called "my both known and faithful friends." It is also suggested that he had long hoped to emigrate to the New World, "... as myself then much desired, and

---

[17] Thomas Prince, *A Chronological History of New England* ... (Boston, 1736), vol. I, pt. 2, p. 71, fn. 38.

shortly hope to effect, if the Lord will, the putting to of my shoulder in this hopeful business."

His letter explains the reasons for the emigration and settlement, and hope that he will soon join the colony himself.

To the Reader

Courteous Reader, be entreated to make a favorable construction of my forwardness in publishing these ensuing discourses. The desire of carrying the Gospel of Christ into those foreign parts, amongst those people that as yet have had no knowledge nor taste of God, as also to procure unto themselves and others a quiet and comfortable habitation, were, amongst other things, the inducements (unto these undertakings of the then hopeful, and now experimentally known good enterprise for plantation in New England) to set afoot and prosecute the same. And though it fared with them, as it is common to the most actions of this nature, that the first attempts prove difficult, as the sequel more at large expresseth, yet it hath pleased God, even beyond our expectation in so short a time, to give hope of letting some of them see (though some he hath taken out of this vale of tears)[18] some grounds of hope of the accomplishment of both those ends by them at first propounded.

And as myself then much desired, and shortly hope to effect, if the Lord will, the putting to of my shoulder in this hopeful business, and in the meantime, these relations coming to my hand from my both known and faithful friends, on whose writings I do much rely, I thought it not amiss to make them more general,

---

[18] The writer studiously avoids mentioning the grim fact that more than half of the group who sailed on the *Mayflower* had already died.

hoping of a cheerful proceeding, both of adventurers and planters, entreating that the example of the honorable Virginia and Bermudas Companies, encountering with so many disasters, and that for divers years together, with an unwearied resolution, the good effects whereof are now eminent, may prevail as a spur of preparation also touching this no less hopeful country, though yet an infant, the extent and commodities whereof are as yet not fully known, after time will unfold more. Such as desire to take knowledge of things, may inform themselves by this ensuing treatise, and, if they please, also by such as have been there a first and second time.[19] My hearty prayer to God is that the event of this and all other honorable and honest undertakings, may be for the furtherance of the kingdom of Christ, the enlarging of the bounds of our sovereign lord King James, and the good and profit of those who, either by purse or person or both, are agents in the same, so I take leave, and rest

Thy friend, G. Mourt.[20]

---

[19] Although they were pioneer settlers in New England, the Pilgrims had not come to unknown territory. This portion of the coast had been sailed by Giovanni de Verrazzano as early as 1524; probably the first Englishman to visit the area was Bartholomew Gosnold in 1602. In 1605, George Weymouth commanded a voyage of exploration and trade, and kidnapped five Indians in Maine, of whom one, Squanto, later befriended the Pilgrims. By 1608, Samuel de Champlain had even charted the *Port du Cap de St. Louis*, which was to become Plymouth Harbor. Capt. John Smith's map of New England, prepared on a voyage in 1614, already shows the site named "Plimouth." Apparently two mates (or pilots?) of the *Mayflower* had sailed the coast previously.

[20] Reasons for assuming that the writer is George Morton have been discussed in the Introduction.

Chapter 4: Letter from Pastor John Robinson

The following letter is an odd addition to this "Relation" or journal, simply because it is a letter written to the members of the colony, instead of written *about* them.

Like Robert Cushman, Pastor John Robinson stayed behind while the settlers sailed on the Mayflower. He had been their pastor since their removal to Holland, and planned to join the Plymouth colony in the future. However, he died in Leyden in 1625.

His letter is one of spiritual encouragement as he knows they will face hardship and frustration in a strange land.

Certain useful advertisements sent in a Letter written by a discreet friend unto the Planters in New England, at their first setting sail from Southampton, who earnestly desireth the prosperity of that their new Plantation.

Loving and Christian friends. I do heartily and in the Lord salute you all, as being they with whom I am present in my best affection, and most earnest longings after you, though I be constrained for a while to be bodily absent from you; I say constrained, God knowing how willingly and much rather than otherwise I would have borne my part with you in this first brunt, were I not by strong necessity held back for the present. Make account of me in the meanwhile, as of a man divided in myself with great pain, and as (natural bonds set aside) having my better part with you.

And though I doubt not but in your godly wisdoms you both foresee and resolve upon that which concerneth your present state and condition, both severally and jointly, yet have I thought but my duty to add some further spur of provocation unto them who run already, if not because you need it, yet because I owe it in love and duty.

And first, as we are daily to renew our repentance with our God, special for our sins known, and general for our unknown trespasses, so doth the Lord call us in a singular manner upon occasions of such difficulty and danger as lieth upon you, to a both more narrow search and careful reformation of our ways in his sight, lest he, calling to remembrance our sins forgotten by us or unrepented of, take advantage against us, and in judgment leave us for the same to be swallowed up in one danger or other; whereas on the contrary, sin being taken away by earnest repentance and pardon thereof from the Lord, sealed up unto a man's conscience by his Spirit, great shall be his security and peace in all dangers, sweet his comforts in all distresses, with happy deliverance from all evil, whether in life or in death.

Now next after this heavenly peace with God and our own consciences, we are carefully to provide for peace with all men what in us lieth, especially with our associates, and for that end watchfulness must be had, that we neither at all in ourselves do give, no, nor easily take offense being given by others. Woe be unto the world for offenses, for though it be necessary (considering the malice of Satan and man's corruption) that offenses come, yet woe unto the man or woman either by whom the offense cometh, saith Christ, Matt. 18:7. And if offenses in the unseasonable use of things in themselves indifferent, be more to be feared than death itself, as the Apostle teacheth, 1 Cor. 9:15, how much more in things simply evil, in which neither honor of God, nor love of man is thought worthy to be regarded.

Neither yet is it sufficient that we keep ourselves by the grace of God from giving offense, except withal we be armed against the taking of them when they are given by others. For how unperfect and lame is the work of grace in that person, who wants charity to cover a multitude of offenses, as the Scriptures speak. Neither are you to be exhorted to this grace only upon the common grounds of Christianity, which are, that persons ready to take offense, either want charity to cover offenses, or wisdom duly to weigh human frailty; or lastly are gross, though close hypocrites, as Christ our Lord teacheth, Matt. 7:1,2,3, as indeed in mine own experience, few or none have been found which sooner give offense, than such as easily take it; neither have they ever proved sound and profitable members in societies, which have nourished in themselves that touchy humor.

But besides these, there are divers special motives provoking you above others to great care and conscience this way: as first, you are many of you strangers, as to the persons, so to the infirmities one of another, and so stand in need of more watchfulness this way, lest when such things fall out in men and women as you suspected not, you be inordinately affected with them, which doth require at your hands much wisdom and charity for the covering and preventing of incident offenses that way. And lastly your intended course of civil community will minister continual occasion of offense, and will be as fuel for that fire, except you diligently quench it with brotherly forbearance. And if taking offense causelessly or easily at men's doings be so carefully to be avoided, how much more heed is to be taken that we take not offense at God himself, which yet we certainly do so oft as we do murmur at his providence in our crosses, or bear impatiently such afflictions as wherewith he pleaseth to visit us. Store we up therefore patience against the evil day, without which we take offense at the Lord himself in his holy and just works.

A fourth thing there is carefully to be provided for, to wit, that with your common employments you join common affections truly bent upon the general good, avoiding as a deadly plague of your both common and special comfort all retiredness of mind for proper advantage, and all singularly affected any manner of way; let every man repress in himself and the whole body in each person, as so many rebels against the common good, all private respects of men's selves, not sorting with the general conveniency. And as men are careful not to have a new house shaken with any violence before it be well settled and the parts firmly knit, so be you, I beseech you brethren, much more careful, that the house of God which you are and are to be, be not shaken with unnecessary novelties or other oppositions at the first settling thereof.

Lastly, whereas you are to become a body politic, using amongst yourselves civil government, and are not furnished with any persons of special eminency above the rest, to be chosen by you into office of government, let your wisdom and godliness appear not only in

44

choosing such persons as do entirely love, and will diligently promote the common good, but also in yielding unto them all due honor and obedience in their lawful administrations, not beholding in them the ordinariness of their persons, but God's ordinance for your good, nor being like unto the foolish multitude, who more honor the gay coat than either the virtuous mind of the man or glorious ordinance of the Lord. But you know better things, and that the image of the Lord's power and authority which the Magistrate beareth is honorable, in how mean persons soever. And this duty you both may the more willingly, and ought the more conscionably to perform, because you are at least for the present to have only them for your ordinary governors which yourselves shall make choice of for that work.

Sundry other things of importance I could put you in mind of, and of those before mentioned in more words, but I will not so far wrong your godly minds as to think you heedless of these things, there being also divers among you so well able to admonish both themselves and others of what concerneth them.

These few things therefore, and the same in few words I do earnestly commend unto your care and conscience, joining therewith my daily incessant prayers unto the Lord, that he who hath made the heavens and the earth, the sea and all rivers of waters, and whose providence is over all his works, especially over all his dear children for good, would so guide and guard you in your ways, as inwardly by his Spirit, so outwardly by the hand of his power, as that both you and we also, for and with you, may have after matter of praising his name all the days of your and our lives. Fare you well in him in whom you trust, and in whom I rest

An unfeigned well-willer
of your happy success
in this hopeful voyage,
I. R.[21]

---

[21] Presumably, the initials of John Robinson, pastor of the Leyden congregation. See Introduction.

Chapter 5: The Pilgrim Journal

Now we come to the "Relation," or journal of the first year in the Plymouth Colony. This journal was kept by William Bradford (who later published his much more detailed *Of Plymouth Plantation*) and Eward Winslow.

This first year was eventful, from the signing of the Mayflower Compact, choosing a settlement location, meeting Squanto, building a town, a great loss of settlers to the "general sickness," making a peace treaty with Massasoit, and the first harvest celebration, or First Thanksgiving.

America (and the world) is forever indebted to these men who chronicled the first successful colony in New England.

A relation or journal of the proceedings of the plantation settled at Plymouth in New England.

Wednesday, the sixth of September, the wind coming east-north-east, a fine small gale, we loosed from Plymouth, having been kindly entertained and courteously used by divers friends there dwelling, and after many difficulties in boisterous storms, at length, by God's providence, upon the ninth of November following, by break of the day we espied land which we deemed to be Cape Cod, and so afterward it proved. And the appearance of it much comforted us, especially seeing so goodly a land, and wooded to the brink of the sea. It caused us to rejoice together, and praise God that had given us once again to see land. And thus we made our course south-south-west, purposing to go to a river ten leagues to the south of the Cape,[22] but at night the wind being contrary, we put round again for the bay of Cape Cod. And upon the 11th of November we came to an anchor in the bay,[23] which is a good harbor and pleasant bay, circled round, except in the entrance which is about four miles over from land to land, compassed about to the very sea with oaks, pines, juniper, sassafras, and other sweet wood.

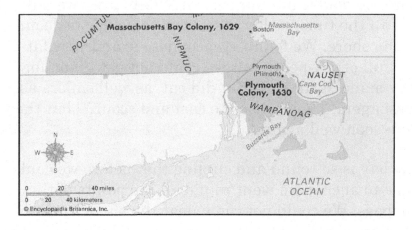

It is a harbor wherein a thousand sail of ships may safely ride. There we relieved ourselves with wood and water, and refreshed our people, while our shallop was fitted to coast the bay, to search for a habitation. There was the greatest store of fowl that ever we saw.

---

[22] Bradford's *Of Plymouth Plantation* identifies this as the Hudson River, where the New Netherlands Company had invited the Pilgrims to settle. Ten leagues appears too short a distance from Cape Cod to the Hudson: *ten* may here be a misprint, or reference may be to the appropriate latitude rather than to the mouth of the river.

[23] Presumably, Provincetown Harbor.

And every day we saw whales playing hard by us, of which in that place, if we had instruments and means to take them, we might have made a very rich return, which to our great grief we wanted. Our master and his mate, and others experienced in fishing, professed we might have made three or four thousand pounds' worth of oil. They preferred it before Greenland whale-fishing, and purpose the next winter to fish for whale here. For cod we assayed, but found none; there is good store, no doubt, in their season. Neither got we any fish all the time we lay there, but some few little ones on the shore. We found great mussels, and very fat and full of sea-pearl, but we could not eat them, for they made us all sick that did eat, as well sailors as passengers. They caused to cast and scour,[24] but they were soon well again.

The bay is so round and circling that before we could come to anchor we went round all the points of the compass. We could not come near the shore by three quarters of an English mile, because of shallow water, which was a great prejudice to us, for our people going on shore were forced to wade a bow shot or two in going a land, which caused many to get colds and coughs, for it was nigh times freezing cold weather.

This day before we came to harbor, observing some not well affected to unity and concord, but gave some appearance of faction,[25] it was thought good there

---

[24] to vomit and have diarrhea

[25] Members of the Leyden congregation were fearful of mutiny and other abuses by some of the many "Strangers" who had joined the group in England. The party had no patent

should be an association and agreement that we should combine together in one body, and to submit to such government and governors as we should by common consent agree to make and choose, and set our hands to this that follows word for word.[26]

> In the name of God, Amen. We whose names are underwritten, the loyal subjects of our dread sovereign lord King James, by the grace of God, of Great Britain, France, and Ireland King, Defender of the Faith, etc.
>
> Having undertaken, for the glory of God, and advancement of the Christian faith, and honor of our king and country, a voyage to plant the first colony in the northern parts of Virginia[27], do by these presents solemnly and mutually in the presence of God and one of another, covenant, and combine ourselves together into a civil body politic, for our better ordering and preservation, and furtherance of the ends aforesaid; and by

---

for New England, so that they would have been a people outside the law as soon as they disembarked, and individual license could have posed a real threat.

[26] This is the earliest known text of the famous "Mayflower Compact", the original document has never been found. John Quincy Adams overstated the case when he said that "This is perhaps the only instance in human history of that positive social compact which speculative philosophers have imagined as the only legitimate source of government." As evidenced in the signatures, the distinction between masters and servants remained, and women had no legal voice but were still chattel. Nevertheless, it is an unusual document in which the concept of self-government emerges so sharply during a time when the divine right of kings was assumed. It is clearly modelled on the "covenants" or "combinations" which characterized most Separatist congregations, and is presaged in Rev. Robinson's farewell letter.

[27] "Virginia" was a general term for much of New England at this time.

virtue hereof to enact, constitute, and frame such just and equal laws, ordinances, acts, constitutions, offices from time to time, as shall be thought most meet and convenient for the general good of the colony: unto which we promise all due submission and obedience. In witness whereof we have hereunder subscribed our names; Cape Cod, the 11th of November, in the year of the reign of our sovereign lord King James, of England, France and Ireland eighteenth and of Scotland fifty-fourth, Anno Domini 1620.[28]

The same day, so soon as we could, we set ashore fifteen or sixteen men, well-armed, with some to fetch wood, for we had none left; as also to see what the land was, and what inhabitants they could meet with. They found it to be a small neck of land, on this side where we lay is the bay, and the further side the sea; the ground or earth, sand hills, much like the downs in Holland, but much better; the crust of the earth a spit's[29] depth excellent black earth; all wooded with oaks, pines, sassafras, juniper, birch, holly, vines,

---

[28] The names of the signers were first printed in Nathaniel Morton's *New England's Memorial* (Cambridge, 1669). In alphabetical order, they are: John Alden, Isaac Allerton, John Allerton, John Billington, William Bradford, William Brewster, Richard Britteridge, Peter Brown, John Carver, James Chilton, Richard Clark, Francis Cook, John Crackstone, Edward Doten, Francis Eaton, Thomas English, Moses Fletcher, Edward Fuller, Samuel Fuller, Richard Gardiner, John Goodman, Stephen Hopkins, John Howland, Edward Leister, Edmond Margeson, Christopher Martin, William Mullins, Digory Priest, John Ridgedale, Thomas Rogers, George Soule, Miles Standish, Edward Tilley, John Tilley, Thomas Tinker, John Turner, Richard Warren, William White, Thomas Williams, Edward Winslow, Gilbert Winslow.

[29] spade's

some ash, walnut; the wood for the most part open and without underwood, fit either to go or ride in. At night our people returned, but found not any person, nor habitation, and laded[30] their boat with juniper, which smelled very sweet and strong and of which we burnt the most part of the time we lay there.

THE SHALLOP, WHICH THE PILGRIMS BROUGHT WITH THEM ON THE MAYFLOWER.

Monday, the 13th of November, we unshipped our shallop[31] and drew her on land, to mend and repair her, having been forced to cut her down in bestowing her betwixt the decks, and she was much opened with the people's lying in her,[32] which kept us long there, for it was sixteen or seventeen days before the carpenter had finished her. Our people went on shore

---

[30] *loaded*

[31] A large longboat which can be rowed, or fitted with a small mast and sails.

[32] An indication of the overcrowded conditions aboard the *Mayflower* is the fact that some passengers slept in the shallop, which had been partially disassembled for easier storage.

to refresh themselves, and our women to wash, as they had great need. But whilst we lay thus still, hoping our shallop would be ready in five or six days at the furthest, but our carpenter made slow work of it, so that some of our people, impatient of delay, desired for our better furtherance to travel by land into the country, which was not without appearance of danger, not having the shallop with them, nor means to carry provision, but on their backs, to see whether it might be fit for us to seat in or no, and the rather because as we sailed into the harbor there seemed to be a river opening itself into the main land. The willingness of the persons was liked, but the thing itself, in regard of the danger, was rather permitted than approved, and so with cautions, directions, and instructions, sixteen men were set out with every man his musket, sword, and corslet, under the conduct of Captain Miles Standish, unto whom was adjoined, for counsel and advice, William Bradford, Stephen Hopkins, and Edward Tilley.

Wednesday, the 15th of November, they were set ashore, and when they had ordered themselves in the order of a single file and marched about the space of a mile, by the sea they espied five or six people with a dog, coming towards them, who were savages, who when they saw them, ran into the wood and whistled the dog after them, etc. First they supposed them to be Master Jones, the master, and some of his men, for they were ashore and knew of their coming, but after they knew them to be Indians they marched after them into the woods, lest other of the Indians should lie in ambush. But when the Indians saw our men following them, they ran away with might and main and our men turned out of the wood after them, for it was the way they intended to go, but they could not come near them. They followed them that night about ten miles by the trace of their footings, and saw how they had come the same way they went, and at a turning perceived how they ran up a hill, to see whether they followed them. At length night came upon them, and they were constrained to take up their lodging, so they set forth three sentinels, and the rest, some kindled a fire, and others fetched wood, and there held our rendezvous that night.

In the morning so soon as we could see the trace, we proceeded on our journey, and had the track until we had compassed the head of a long creek, and there they took into another wood, and we after them, supposing to find some of their dwellings, but we marched through boughs and bushes, and under hills and valleys, which tore our very armor in pieces, and yet could meet with none of them, nor their houses, nor find any fresh water, which we greatly desired, and stood in need of, for we brought neither beer nor water with us, and our victuals was only biscuit and Holland cheese, and a little bottle of aquavitae[33], so as we were sore athirst. About ten o'clock we came into a deep valley, full of brush, wood-gaile, and long grass, through which we found little paths or tracks, and there we saw a deer, and found springs of fresh water,

---

[33] *An alcoholic drink*

of which we were heartily glad, and sat us down and drunk our first New England water with as much delight as ever we drunk drink in all our lives.

When we had refreshed ourselves, we directed our course full south, that we might come to the shore, which within a short while after we did, and there made a fire, that they in the ship might see where we were (as we had direction) and so marched on towards this supposed river. And as we went in another valley we found a fine clear pond of fresh water, being about a musket shot broad and twice as long. There grew also many fine vines, and fowl and deer haunted there; there grew much sassafras.[34] From thence we went on, and found much plain ground, about fifty acres, fit for the plow, and some signs where the Indians had formerly planted their corn. After this, some thought it best, for nearness of the river, to go down and travel on the sea sands, by which means some of our men were tired, and lagged behind. So we stayed and gathered them up, and struck into the land again, where we found a little path to certain heaps of sand, one whereof was covered with old mats, and had a wooden thing like a mortar whelmed[35] on the top of it, and an earthen pot laid in a little hole at the end thereof. We, musing what it might be, digged and found a bow, and, as we thought, arrows, but they were rotten. We supposed there were many other

---

[34] The frequent mention of sassafras is understandable in view of the immense commercial value of that plant in the early seventeenth century; the root and bark were sold as medicines throughout the Old World.

[35] overturned

things, but because we deemed them graves, we put in the bow again and made it up as it was, and left the rest untouched, because we thought it would be odious unto them to ransack their sepulchers.

We went on further and found new stubble, of which they had gotten corn this year, and many walnut trees full of nuts, and great store of strawberries, and some vines. Passing thus a field or two, which were not great, we came to another which had also been new gotten, and there we found where a house had been, and four or five old planks laid together; also we found a great kettle which had been some ship's kettle and brought out of Europe.[36] There was also a heap of sand, made like the former—but it was newly done, we might see how they had paddled it with their hands— which we digged up, and in it we found a little old basket full of fair Indian corn, and digged further and found a fine great new basket full of very fair corn of this year, with some thirty-six goodly ears of corn, some yellow, and some red, and others mixed with blue, which was a very goodly sight. The basket was round, and narrow at the top; it held about three or four bushels, which was as much as two of us could lift up from the ground, and was very handsomely and cunningly made. But whilst we were busy about these things, we set our men sentinel in a round ring, all but two or three which digged up the corn. We were in suspense what to do with it and the kettle, and at length, after much consultation, we concluded to take

---

[36] Cf. note 2, p. 16.

57

the kettle and as much of the corn as we could carry away with us; and when our shallop came, if we could find any of the people, and come to parley with them, we would give them the kettle again, and satisfy them for their corn.[37] So we took all the ears, and put a good deal of the loose corn in the kettle for two men to bring away on a staff; besides, they that could put any into their pockets filled the same. The rest we buried again, for we were so laden with armor that we could carry no more.

Not far from this place we found the remainder of an old fort, or palisade, which as we conceived had been made by some Christians. This was also hard by that place which we thought had been a river, unto which we went and found it so to be, dividing itself into two arms by a high bank. Standing right by the cut or mouth which came from the sea, that which was next unto us was the less; the other arm was more than twice as big, and not unlike to be a harbor for ships. But whether it be a fresh river, or only an indraught of the sea, we had no time to discover, for we had commandment to be out but two days. Here also we saw two canoes, the one on the one side, the other on the other side; we could not believe it was a canoe, till we came near it. So we returned, leaving the further discovery hereof to our shallop, and came that night back again to the fresh water pond, and there we made our rendezvous that night, making a great fire, and a

---

[37] It is little wonder that the Indians later took the Pilgrims to task for having appropriated dried corn from such caches where it had been stored.

barricade to windward of us, and kept good watch with three sentinels all night, every one standing when his turn came, while five or six inches of match was burning.[38] It proved a very rainy night.

Matchlock musket, c. 1600

In the morning we took our kettle and sunk it in the pond, and trimmed our muskets, for few of them would go off because of the wet, and so coasted the wood again to come home, in which we were shrewdly puzzled, and lost our way. As we wandered we came to a tree, where a young sprit[39] was bowed down over a bow, and some acorns strewed underneath. Stephen Hopkins said it had been to catch some deer. So as we were looking at it, William Bradford being in the rear, when he came looked also upon it, and as he went about, it gave a sudden jerk up, and he was immediately caught by the leg. It was a very pretty device, made with a rope of their own making and having a noose as artificially[40] made as any roper in England can make, and as like ours as can be, which we brought away with us. In the end we got out of the wood, and were fallen about a mile too high above the

---

[38] Most of their guns were matchlocks.

[39] sapling

[40] artfully; skillfully

creek, where we saw three bucks, but we had rather have had one of them.[41] We also did spring three couple of partridges, and as we came along by the creek we saw great flocks of wild geese and ducks, but they were very fearful of us. So we marched some while in the woods, some while on the sands, and other while in the water up to the knees, till at length we came near the ship, and then we shot off our pieces, and the long boat came to fetch us. Master Jones and Master Carver being on the shore, with many of our people, came to meet us. And thus we came both weary and welcome home, and delivered in our corn into the store, to be kept for seed, for we knew not how to come by any, and therefore were very glad, purposing, so soon as we could meet with any of the inhabitants of that place, to make them large satisfaction. This was our first discovery, whilst our shallop was in repairing.

Our people did make things as fitting as they could, and time would, in seeking out wood, and helving[42] of tools, and sawing of timber to build a new shallop. But the discommodiousness of the harbor did much hinder us for we could neither go to nor come from the shore, but at high water, which was much to our hindrance and hurt, for oftentimes they waded to the middle of the thigh, and oft to the knees, to go and come from land. Some did it necessarily, and some for their own pleasure, but it brought to the most, if not to all, coughs and colds, the weather proving suddenly cold

---

[41] A quaint touch of humor.
[42] hafting

and stormy, which afterwards turned to the scurvy,[43] whereof many died.

When our shallop was fit—indeed, before she was fully fitted, for there was two days' work after bestowed on her—there was appointed some twenty-four men of our own, and armed, then to go and make a more full discovery of the rivers before mentioned. Master Jones[44] was desirous to go with us, and we took such of his sailors as he thought useful for us, so as we were in all about thirty-four men. We made Master Jones our leader, for we thought it best herein to gratify his kindness and forwardness. When we were set forth, it proved rough weather and cross winds, so as we were constrained, some in the shallop, and others in the long boat, to row to the nearest shore the wind would suffer them to go unto, and then to wade out above the knees. The wind was so strong as the shallop could not keep the water, but was forced to harbor there that night, but we marched six or seven miles further, and appointed the shallop to come to us as soon as they could. It blowed and did snow all that day and night, and froze withal; some of our people that are dead took the original of their death here.

The next day, about eleven o'clock, our shallop came to us and we shipped ourselves, and the wind being good, we sailed to the river we formerly discovered, which we named Cold Harbor, to which when we came we

---

[43] More likely, pneumonia.
[44] *Not one of the Pilgrims, but the sailor*

found it not navigable for ships, yet we thought it might be a good harbor for boats, for it flows there twelve foot at high water. We landed our men between the two creeks and marched some four or five miles by the greater of them, and the shallop followed us. At length night grew on, and our men were tired with marching up and down the steep hills and deep valleys which lay half a foot thick with snow. Master Jones, wearied with marching, was desirous we should take up our lodging, though some of us would have marched further, so we made there our rendezvous for that night, under a few pine trees. And as it fell out, we got three fat geese and six ducks to our supper, which we ate with soldiers' stomachs, for we had eaten little all that day. Our resolution was next morning to go up to the head of this river, for we supposed it would prove fresh water, but in the morning our resolution held not, because many liked not the hilliness of the soil, and badness of the harbor. So we turned towards the other creek, that we might go over and look for the rest of the corn that we left behind when we were here before.

When we came to the creek we saw the canoe lie on the dry ground, and a flock of geese in the river, at which one made a shot and killed a couple of them, and we launched the canoe and fetched them and when we had done, she carried us over by seven or eight at once. This done, we marched to the place where we had the corn formerly, which place we called Cornhill, and digged and found the rest, of which we were very glad. We also digged in a place a little further off, and found a bottle of oil. We went to another place which we had seen before, and digged, and found more corn, viz. two or three baskets full of Indian wheat,[45] and a bag of beans, with a good many of fair wheat ears. Whilst some of us were digging up this, some others found another heap of corn, which they digged up also, so as we had in all about ten bushels, which will serve us sufficiently for seed. **Note:** And sure it was God's good providence that we found this corn, for else we know not how we should have done, for we knew not how we should find or meet with any Indians, except it be to do us a mischief.[46] Also, we had never in all likelihood seen a grain of it if we had not made our first journey, for the ground was now covered with snow, and so hard frozen that we were fain with our cutlasses and short swords to hew and carve the ground a foot deep, and then wrest it up with levers, for we had forgot to bring other tools. Whilst we were in this employment, foul weather being towards, Master Jones was earnest to go aboard, but sundry of us desired to make further discovery and to find out the Indians' habitations. So we sent home with him our weakest people, and some that were sick, and all the corn, and eighteen of us stayed still, and lodged there that night, and desired that the shallop might return to us next day and bring us some mattocks and spades with them.

---

[45] I.e., corn.

[46] Knowledge of Indian attacks on white settlers in the Spanish colonies and in what is now Virginia had led the Pilgrims to expect ill of them.

The next morning we followed certain beaten paths and tracks of the Indians into the woods, supposing they would have led us into some town, or houses. After we had gone a while, we light upon a very broad beaten path, well nigh two feet broad. Then we lighted all our matches[47] and prepared ourselves, concluding that we were near their dwellings, but in the end we found it to be only a path made to drive deer in, when the Indians hunt, as we supposed.

When we had marched five or six miles into the woods and could find no signs of any people, we returned again another way, and as we came into the plain ground we found a place like a grave, but it was much bigger and longer than any we had yet seen. It was also covered with boards, so as we mused what it should be, and resolved to dig it up, where we found, first a mat, and under that a fair bow, and there another mat, and under that a board about three quarters[48] long, finely carved and painted, with three tines, or broaches, on the top, like a crown. Also between the mats we found bowls, trays, dishes, and such like trinkets. At length we came to a fair new mat, and under that two bundles, the one bigger, the other less. We opened the greater and found in it a great quantity of fine and perfect red powder, and in it the bones and skull of a man. The skull had fine yellow hair still on it, and some of the flesh unconsumed;

---

[47] I.e., the slow-burning wicks of their matchlock muskets.

[48] [of a yard]

there was bound up with it a knife, a packneedle,[49] and two or three old iron things. It was bound up in a sailor's canvas cassock, and a pair of cloth breeches. The red powder was a kind of embalment, and yielded a strong, but no offensive smell; it was as fine as any flour. We opened the less bundle likewise, and found of the same powder in it, and the bones and head of a little child. About the legs and other parts of it was bound strings and bracelets of fine white beads; there was also by it a little bow, about three quarters long, and some other odd knacks. We brought sundry of the prettiest things away with us, and covered the corpse up again. After this, we digged in sundry like places, but found no more corn, nor any thing else but graves.

There was variety of opinions amongst us about the embalmed person. Some thought it was an Indian lord and king. Others said the Indians have all black hair, and never any was seen with brown or yellow hair. Some thought it was a Christian of some special note, which had died amongst them, and they thus buried him to honor him. Others thought they had killed him, and did it in triumph over him.

Whilst we were thus ranging and searching, two of the sailors, which were newly come on the shore, by chance espied two houses which had been lately dwelt in, but the people were gone. They, having their pieces and hearing nobody, entered the houses and took out

_____

[49] a large strong needle used for sewing packages in stout cloth

some things, and durst not stay but came again and told us. So some seven or eight of us went with them, and found how we had gone within a flight shot of them before. The houses were made with long young sapling trees, bended and both ends stuck into the ground. They were made round, like unto an arbor, and covered down to the ground with thick and well wrought mats, and the door was not over a yard high, made of a mat to open. The chimney was a wide open hole in the top, for which they had a mat to cover it close when they pleased. One might stand and go upright in them. In the midst of them were four little trunches[50] knocked into the ground, and small sticks laid over, on which they hung their pots, and what they had to seethe.[51] Round about the fire they lay on mats, which are their beds. The houses were double matted, for as they were matted without, so were they within, with newer and fairer mats. In the houses we found wooden bowls, trays and dishes, earthen pots, handbaskets made of crabshells wrought together, also an English pail or bucket; it wanted a bail, but it had two iron ears. There was also baskets of sundry sorts, bigger and some lesser, finer and some coarser; some were curiously wrought with black and white in pretty works, and sundry other of their household stuff. We found also two or three deer's heads, one whereof had been newly killed, for it was still fresh. There was also a company of deer's feet stuck up in the houses, harts' horns, and eagles' claws, and sundry such like things

---

[50] stakes

[51] simmer; boil

there was, also two or three baskets full of parched acorns, pieces of fish, and a piece of a broiled herring. We found also a little silk grass, and a little tobacco seed, with some other seeds which we knew not. Without was sundry bundles of flags, and sedge, bulrushes, and other stuff to make mats. There was thrust into a hollow tree two or three pieces of venison, but we thought it fitter for the dogs than for us. Some of the best things we took away with us, and left the houses standing still as they were.

So it growing towards night, and the tide almost spent, we hasted with our things down to the shallop, and got aboard that night, intending to have brought some beads and other things to have left in the houses, in sign of peace and that we meant to truck with them, but it was not done, by means of our hasty coming away from Cape Cod. But so soon as we can meet conveniently with them, we will give them full satisfaction. Thus much of our second discovery.

Having thus discovered this place, it was controversial amongst us what to do touching our abode and settling there; some thought it best, for many reasons, to abide there.

As first, that there was a convenient harbor for boats, though not for ships.

Secondly, good corn-ground ready to our hands, as we saw by experience in the goodly corn it yielded, which would again agree with the ground, and be natural seed for the same.

Thirdly, Cape Cod was like to be a place of good fishing, for we saw daily great whales of the best kind for oil and bone, come close aboard our ship, and in fair weather swim and play about us. There was once one, when the sun shone warm, came and lay above water as if she had been dead, for a good while together, within half a musket shot of the ship, at which two were prepared to shoot to see whether she would stir or no. He that gave fire first, his musket flew in pieces, both stock and barrel, yet, thanks be to God, neither he nor any man else was hurt with it, though many were there about. But when the whale saw her time, she gave a snuff, and away.

Fourthly, the place was likely to be healthful, secure, and defensible.

But the last and especial reason was, that now the heart of winter and unseasonable weather was come upon us, so that we could not go upon coasting and discovery without danger of losing men and boat, upon which would follow the overthrow of all, especially considering what variable winds and sudden storms do there arise. Also, cold and wet lodging had so tainted our people, for scarce any of us were free from vehement coughs, as if they should continue long in that estate it would endanger the lives of many, and breed diseases and infection amongst us. Again, we had yet some beer, butter, flesh, and other such victuals left, which would quickly be all gone, and then we should have nothing to comfort us in the great labor and toil we were like to undergo at the first. It was also conceived, whilst we had competent victuals, that the ship would stay with us, but when that grew low, they would be gone and let us shift as we could.

Others again, urged greatly the going to Anguum, or Angoum,[52] a place twenty leagues off to the northwards, which they had heard to be an excellent harbor for ships, better ground, and better fishing. Secondly, for anything we knew, there might be hard by us a far better seat, and it should be a great hindrance to seat where we should remove again. Thirdly, the water was but in ponds, and it was thought there would be none in summer, or very little. Fourthly, the water there must be fetched up a steep hill. But to omit many reasons and replies used hereabouts, it was in the end concluded to make some discovery within the bay, but in no case so far as Anguum. Besides, Robert Coppin, our pilot, made relation of a great navigable river and good harbor in the other headland of this bay, almost right over against Cape Cod, being in a right line not much above eight leagues distant, in which he had been once; and because that one of the wild men with whom they had some trucking stole a harping iron[53] from them, they called it Thievish Harbor. And beyond that place they were enjoined not to go, whereupon, a company was chosen to go out upon a third discovery. Whilst some

---

[52] Agawam; now, Ipswich, Massachusetts.
[53] harpoon

69

were employed in this discovery, it pleased God that Mistress White was brought a-bed of a son, which was called Peregrine.

The 5th day, we, through God's mercy, escaped a great danger by the foolishness of a boy, one of Francis Billington's sons, who, in his father's absence, had got gunpowder and had shot off a piece or two, and made squibs[54], and there being a fowling-piece charged in his father's cabin, shot her off in the cabin; there being a little barrel of powder half full, scattered in and about the cabin, the fire being within four feet of the bed between the decks, and many flints and iron things about the cabin, and many people about the fire, and yet, by God's mercy, no harm done.

Wednesday, the 6th of December, it was resolved our discoverers should set forth, for the day before was too foul weather, and so they did, though it was well o'er the day ere all things could be ready. So ten of our men were appointed who were of themselves willing to undertake it, to wit, Captain Standish, Master Carver, William Bradford, Edward Winslow, John Tilley, Edward Tilley, John Howland, and three of London: Richard Warren, Stephen Hopkins, and Edward Dotte; and two of our seamen: John Allerton and Thomas English. Of the ship's company there went two of the master's mates, Master Clarke and Master Coppin, the master gunner, and three sailors. The narration of

---

[54] *a small firework that burns with a hissing sound before exploding*

which discovery follows, penned by one of the company.

Wednesday, the 6th of December, we set out, being very cold and hard weather. We were a long while after we launched from the ship before we could get clear of a sandy point which lay within less than a furlong of the same. In which time two were very sick, and Edward Tilley had like to have sounded[55] with cold; the gunner also was sick unto death, (but hope of trucking made him to go), and so remained all that day and the next night. At length we got clear of the sandy point and got up our sails, and within an hour or two we got under the weather shore, and then had smoother water and better sailing, but it was very cold, for the water froze on our clothes and made them many times like coats of iron. We sailed six or seven leagues by the shore, but saw neither river nor creek; at length we met with a tongue of land, being flat off from the shore, with a sandy point. We bore up to gain the point, and found there a fair income or road of a bay, being a league over at the narrowest, and some two or three in length, but we made right over to the land before us, and left the discovery of this income till the next day. As we drew near to the shore, we espied some ten or twelve Indians very busy about a black thing—what it was we could not tell—till afterwards they saw us, and ran to and fro as if they had been carrying something away. We landed a league or two

---

[55] swooned

from them, and had much ado to put ashore anywhere, it lay so full of flat sands. When we came to shore, we made us a barricade, and got firewood, and set out our sentinels, and betook us to our lodging, such as it was. We saw the smoke of the fire which the savages made that night, about four or five miles from us.

In the morning we divided our company, some eight in the shallop, and the rest on the shore went to discover this place, but we found it only to be a bay, without either river or creek coming into it. Yet we deemed it to be as good a harbor as Cape Cod, for they that sounded it found a ship might ride in five fathom[56] water. We on the land found it to be a level soil, though none of the fruitfullest. We saw two becks[57] of fresh water, which were the first running streams that we saw in the country, but one might stride over them. We found also a great fish, called a grampus, dead on the sands; they in the shallop found two of them also in the bottom of the bay, dead in like sort. They were cast up at high water, and could not get off for the frost and ice. They were some five or six paces long, and about two inches thick of fat, and fleshed like a swine; they would have yielded a great deal of oil if there had been time and means to have taken it. So we finding nothing for our turn, both we and our shallop returned.

---

[56] *30 feet deep*
[57] brooks

We then directed our course along the sea sands, to the place where we first saw the Indians. When we were there, we saw it was also a grampus which they were cutting up; they cut it into long rands or pieces, about an ell[58] long, and two handful broad. We found here and there a piece scattered by the way, as it seemed, for haste. This place the most were minded we should call the Grampus Bay, because we found so many of them there. We followed the track of the Indians' bare feet a good way on the sands; at length we saw where they struck into the woods by the side of a pond. As we went to view the place, one said he thought he saw an Indian house among the trees, so went up to see. And here we and the shallop lost sight one of another till night, it being now about nine or ten o'clock.

So we light on a path, but saw no house, and followed a great way into the woods. At length we found where corn had been set, but not that year. Anon we found a great burying place, one part whereof was encompassed with a large palisade, like a churchyard, with young spires[59] four or five yards long, set as close one by another as they could, two or three feet in the ground. Within it was full of graves, some bigger and some less; some were also paled about, and others had like an Indian house made over them, but not matted. Those graves were more sumptuous than those at Cornhill, yet we digged none of them up, but only viewed them, and went our way. Without the palisade

---

[58] I.e., 45 inches.
[59] saplings

were graves also, but not so costly. From this place we went and found more corn-ground, but not of this year. As we ranged we light on four or five Indian houses, which had been lately dwelt in, but they were uncovered, and had no mats about them, else they were like those we found at Cornhill but had not been so lately dwelt in. There was nothing left but two or three pieces of old mats, and a little sedge. Also, a little further we found two baskets full of parched acorns hid in the ground, which we supposed had been corn when we began to dig the same; we cast earth thereon again and went our way. All this while we saw no people.

We went ranging up and down till the sun began to draw low, and then we hasted out of the woods, that we might come to our shallop, which when we were out of the woods, we espied a great way off, and called them to come unto us, the which they did as soon as they could, for it was not yet high water. They were exceeding glad to see us (for they feared because they had not seen us in so long a time), thinking we would have kept by the shore side. So being both weary and faint, for we had eaten nothing all that day, we fell to make our rendezvous and get firewood, which always costs us a great deal of labor. By that time we had done, and our shallop come to us, it was within night, and we fed upon such victuals as we had, and betook us to our rest, after we had set out our watch. About midnight we heard a great and hideous cry, and our sentinels called, "Arm! Arm!" So we bestirred ourselves and shot off a couple of muskets, and the noise ceased; we concluded that it was a company of wolves or foxes, for one told us he had heard such a noise in Newfoundland.

About five o'clock in the morning we began to be stirring, and two or three which doubted whether their pieces would go off or no made trial of them, and shot them off, but thought nothing at all. After prayer we prepared ourselves for breakfast and for a journey, and it being now the twilight in the morning, it was thought meet to carry the things down to the shallop. Some said it was not best to carry the armor down; others said they would be readier; two or three said they would not carry theirs till they went themselves, but mistrusting nothing at all. As it fell out, the water not being high enough, they laid the things down upon the shore and came up to breakfast. Anon, all upon a sudden, we heard a great and strange cry, which we knew to be the same voices, though they varied their notes. One of our company, being abroad, came running in and cried, "They are men! Indians! Indians!" and withal, their arrows came flying amongst us.

Our first combat with the Indians.

Our men ran out with all speed to recover their arms, as by the good providence of God they did. In the meantime, Captain Miles Standish, having a snaphance[60] ready, made a shot, and after him

---

[60] A kind of flintlock musket.

another. After they two had shot, other two of us were ready, but he wished us not to shoot till we could take aim, for we knew not what need we should have, and there were four only of us which had their arms there ready, and stood before the open side of our barricade, which was first assaulted. They thought it best to defend it, lest the enemy should take it and our stuff, and so have the more vantage against us. Our care was no less for the shallop, but we hoped all the rest would defend it; we called unto them to know how it was with them, and they answered, "Well! Well!" everyone and, "Be of good courage!" We heard three of their pieces go off, and the rest called for a firebrand to light their matches. One took a log out of the fire on his shoulder and went and carried it unto them, which was thought did not a little discourage our enemies. The cry of our enemies was dreadful, especially when our men ran out to recover their arms; their note was after this manner, *"Woach woach ha ha hach woach."*[61] Our men were no sooner come to their arms, but the enemy was ready to assault them.

There was a lusty man and no whit less valiant, who was thought to be their captain, stood behind a tree within half a musket shot of us, and there let his arrows fly at us. He was seen to shoot three arrows, which were all avoided, for he at whom the first arrow was aimed, saw it, and stooped down and it flew over

---

[61] This defies translation. It is probably less an accurate transcription of specific Algonquian words than an Englishman's vague approximation of the incomprehensible sounds which seemed threatening to him in such a context.

him; the rest were avoided also. He stood three shots of a musket. At length one took, as he said, full aim at him, after which he gave an extraordinary cry and away they went all. We followed them about a quarter of a mile, but we left six to keep our shallop, for we were careful of our business. Then we shouted all together two several times, and shot off a couple of muskets and so returned; this we did that they might see we were not afraid of them nor discouraged.

Thus it pleased God to vanquish our enemies and give us deliverance. By their noise we could not guess that they were less than thirty or forty, though some thought that they were many more. Yet in the dark of the morning we could not so well discern them among the trees, as they could see us by our fireside. We took up eighteen of their arrows which we have sent to England by Master Jones, some whereof were headed with brass, others with harts' horn, and others with eagles' claws. Many more no doubt were shot, for these we found were almost covered with leaves; yet, by the especial providence of God, none of them either hit or hurt us though many came close by us and on every side of us, and some coats which hung up in our barricade were shot through and through.

So after we had given God thanks for our deliverance, we took our shallop and went on our journey, and called this place, The First Encounter. From thence we intended to have sailed to the aforesaid Thievish Harbor, if we found no convenient harbor by the way. Having the wind good, we sailed all that day along the coast about fifteen leagues, but saw neither river nor creek to put into. After we had sailed an hour or two, it began to snow and rain, and to be bad weather. About the midst of the afternoon, the wind increased and the seas began to be very rough, and the hinges of the rudder broke so that we could steer no longer with it, but two men with much ado were fain to serve with a couple of oars. The seas were grown so great that we were much troubled and in great danger, and night grew on. Anon Master Coppin bade us be of good cheer; he saw the harbor. As we drew near, the gale being stiff and we bearing great sail to get in, split our mast in three pieces, and were like to have cast away our shallop. Yet, by God's mercy, recovering ourselves, we had the flood with us, and struck into the harbor.

Now he that thought that had been the place was deceived, it being a place where not any of us had been before, and coming into the harbor, he that was our pilot did bear up northward, which if we had continued we had been cast away. Yet still the Lord kept us, and we bore up for an island before us, and recovering of that island, being compassed about with many rocks, and dark night growing upon us, it pleased the Divine Providence that we fell upon a place of sandy ground, where our shallop did ride safe and secure all that night, and coming upon a strange island kept our watch all night in the rain upon that island. And in the morning we marched about it and found no inhabitants at all, and here we made our rendezvous all that day, being Saturday, 10th of December. On the Sabbath day we rested, and on Monday we sounded the harbor, and found it a very good harbor for our shipping. We marched also into the land, and found divers cornfields, and little running brooks, a place very good for situation, so we returned to our ship again with good news to the rest of our people, which did much comfort their hearts.[62]

On the 15th day we weighed anchor, to go to the place we had discovered, and coming within two leagues of the land, we could not fetch the harbor, but were fain to put room again towards Cape Cod, our course lying west, and the wind was at northwest. But it pleased God that the next day, being Saturday the 16th day, the wind came fair and we put to sea again, and came safely into a safe harbor; and within half an hour the wind changed, so as if we had been letted[63] but a little, we had gone back to Cape Cod.

This harbor is a bay greater than Cape Cod, compassed with a goodly land, and in the bay, two fine islands uninhabited, wherein are nothing but wood, oaks, pines, walnuts, beech, sassafras, vines, and other trees which we know not. This bay is a most hopeful place, innumerable store of fowl, and excellent good, and cannot but be of fish in their seasons; skote,[64] cod, turbot, and herring, we have tasted of, abundance of

---

[62] The landing at Plymouth is reported here as having been almost fortuitous, although some scholars believe that a few of the leaders may long before have planned to settle at that site. Clearly there is nothing here that can be construed as referring to "Plymouth Rock."

[63] hindered

[64] Presumably a misprint for *skate*.

mussels the greatest and best that ever we saw; crabs and lobsters, in their time infinite. It is in fashion like a sickle or fish-hook.

Monday the 18th day, we went a-land, manned with the master of the ship and three or four of the sailors. We marched along the coast in the woods some seven or eight miles, but saw not an Indian nor an Indian house; only we found where formerly had been some inhabitants, and where they had planted their corn. We found not any navigable river, but four or five small running brooks of very sweet fresh water, that all run into the sea. The land for the crust of the earth is, a spit's depth, excellent black mould, and fat[65] in some places, two or three great oaks but not very thick, pines, walnuts, beech, ash, birch, hazel, holly, asp,[66] sassafras in abundance, and vines everywhere, cherry trees, plum trees, and many others which we know not. Many kinds of herbs we found here in winter, as strawberry leaves innumerable, sorrel, yarrow, carvel, brooklime, liverwort, watercresses, great store of leeks and onions, and an excellent strong kind of flax and hemp. Here is sand, gravel, and excellent clay, no better in the world, excellent for pots, and will wash like soap, and great store of stone, though somewhat soft, and the best water that ever we drank, and the brooks now begin to be full of fish. That

---

[65] fertile; rich

[66] aspen

night, many being weary with marching, we went aboard again.

The next morning, being Tuesday the 19th of December, we went again to discover further; some went on land, and some in the shallop. The land we found as the former day we did, and we found a creek, and went up three English miles. A very pleasant river, at full sea a bark of thirty tons may go up, but at low water scarce our shallop could pass. This place we had a great liking to plant in, but that it was so far from our fishing, our principal profit,[67] and so encompassed with woods that we should be in much danger of the savages, and our number being so little, and so much ground to clear, so as we thought good to quit and clear that place till we were of more strength. Some of us having a good mind for safety to plant in the greater isle,[68] we crossed the bay which is there five or six miles over, and found the isle about a mile and a half or two miles about, all wooded, and no fresh water but two or three pits, that we doubted of fresh water in summer, and so full of wood as we could hardly clear so much as to serve us for corn. Besides, we judged it cold for our corn, and some part very

---

[67] The Pilgrims were in a situation far different from that of later pioneers who settled elsewhere as independent farmers. According to the terms of their stringent contract with the "merchant adventurers," their primary concern was to produce salable goods (e.g., fish, lumber, furs) for their sponsors. This commitment was to endure seven years, during which the sponsors were to continue their support of the settlers. The English businessmen seem to have taken full advantage of the dependent situation of the Pilgrims who had no other sources of supply nor outlets for their goods.

[68] Clark's Island, in Plymouth Harbor.

rocky, yet divers[69] thought of it as a place defensible, and of great security.

That night we returned again a-shipboard, with resolution the next morning to settle on some of those places; so in the morning, after we had called on God for direction, we came to this resolution: to go presently ashore again, and to take a better view of two places, which we thought most fitting for us, for we could not now take time for further search or consideration, our victuals being much spent, especially our beer, and it being now the 19th of December. After our landing and viewing of the places, so well as we could we came to a conclusion, by most voices, to set on the mainland, on the first place, on a high ground, where there is a great deal of land cleared, and hath been planted with corn three or four years ago, and there is a very sweet brook runs under the hill side, and many delicate springs of as good water as can be drunk, and where we may harbor our shallops and boats exceeding well, and in this brook much good fish in their seasons; on the further side of the river also much corn-ground cleared. In one field is a great hill on which we point to make a platform and plant our ordnance, which will command all round about. From thence we may see into the bay, and far into the sea, and we may see thence Cape Cod. Our greatest labor will be fetching of our wood, which is half a quarter of an English mile, but there is enough so far off. What people inhabit here we yet know not,

[69] *Meaning "several"*

82

for as yet we have seen none. So there we made our rendezvous, and a place for some of our people, about twenty, resolving in the morning to come all ashore and to build houses.

But the next morning, being Thursday the 21st of December, it was stormy and wet, that we could not go ashore, and those that remained there all night could do nothing, but were wet, not having daylight enough to make them a sufficient court of guard[70] to keep them dry. All that night it blew and rained extremely; it was so tempestuous that the shallop could not go on land so soon as was meet, for they had no victuals on land. About eleven o'clock the shallop went off with much ado with provision, but could not return; it blew so strong and was such foul weather that we were forced to let fall our anchor and ride with three anchors ahead.

Friday, the 22nd, the storm still continued, that we could not get a-land nor they come to us aboard. This morning good-wife[71] Allerton was delivered of a son, but dead born.

Saturday, the 23rd, so many of us as could, went on shore, felled and carried timber, to provide themselves stuff for building.

Sunday, the 24th, our people on shore heard a cry of some savages (as they thought) which caused an

---

[70] guard-house; i.e., a shelter affording some security against possible attack
[71] mistress of a household, (a title of respect)

alarm, and to stand on their guard, expecting an assault, but all was quiet.

Monday, the 25th day[72], we went on shore, some to fell timber, some to saw, some to rive, and some to carry, so no man rested all that day. But towards night some, as they were at work, heard a noise of some Indians, which caused us all to go to our muskets, but we heard no further. So we came aboard again, and left some twenty to keep the court of guard. That night we had a sore storm of wind and rain.

Monday, the 25th day, we went on shore, some to fell drink water aboard, but at night the master caused us to have some beer, and so on board we had divers times now and then some beer, but on shore none at all.

Tuesday, the 26th, it was foul weather, that we could not go ashore.

Wednesday, the 27th, we went to work again.

Thursday, the 28th of December, so many as could went to work on the hill where we purposed to build our platform for our ordnance, and which doth command all the plain and the bay, and from whence we may see far into the sea, and might be easier impaled, having two rows of houses and a fair street. So in the afternoon we went to measure out the grounds, and first we took notice how many families

---

[72] *Christmas Day*

84

there were, willing all single men that had no wives to join with[73] some family, as they thought fit, that so we might build fewer houses, which was done, and we reduced them to nineteen families. To greater[74] families we allotted larger plots, to every person half a pole in breadth, and three in length,[75] and so lots were cast where every man should lie, which was done, and staked out. We thought this proportion was large enough at the first for houses and gardens, to impale them round, considering the weakness of our people, many of them growing ill with cold, for our former discoveries in frost and storms, and the wading at Cape Cod had brought much weakness amongst us, which increased so every day more and more, and after was the cause of many of their deaths.

Friday and Saturday, we fitted ourselves for our labor, but our people on shore were much troubled and discouraged with rain and wet, that day being very stormy and cold. We saw great smokes of fire made by the Indians, about six or seven miles from us, as we conjectured.

Monday, the 1st of January[76], we went betimes to work. We were much hindered in lying so far off from the land, and fain to go as the tide served, that we lost much time, for our ship drew so much water[77] that she

---

[73] *Live with*

[74] *larger*

[75] I.e., 8¼ by 49½ feet.

[76] *1621*

[77] The *Mayflower* was a vessel of 180 tons.

lay a mile and almost a half off, though a ship of seventy or eighty tons at high water may come to the shore.

Wednesday, the 3rd of January, some of our people being abroad to get and gather thatch, they saw great fires of the Indians, and were at their corn-fields, yet saw none of the savages, nor had seen any of them since we came to this bay.

Thursday, the 4th of January, Captain Miles Standish with four or five more, went to see if they could meet with any of the savages in that place where the fires were made. They went to some of their houses, but not lately inhabited, yet could they not meet with any. As they came home, they shot at an eagle and killed her, which was excellent meat; it was hardly to be discerned from mutton.

Friday, the 5th of January, one of the sailors found alive upon the shore a herring, which the master had to his supper, which put us in hope of fish, but as yet we had got but one cod; we wanted small hooks.

Saturday, the 6th of January, Master Martin was very sick, and to our judgment no hope of life, so Master Carver was sent for to come aboard to speak with him about his accounts, who came the next morning.

Monday, the 8th day of January, was a very fair day, and we went betimes to work. Master Jones sent the shallop, as he had formerly done, to see where fish could be got. They had a great storm at sea, and were in some danger; at night they returned with three great seals and an excellent good cod, which did assure us that we should have plenty of fish shortly.

This day, Francis Billington, having the week before seen from the top of a tree on a high hill a great sea as he thought, went with one of the master's mates to see it. They went three miles and then came to a great water, divided into two great lakes, the bigger of them five or six miles in circuit, and in it an isle of a cable length[78] square, the other three miles in compass; in their estimation they are fine fresh water, full of fish, and fowl. A brook issues from it; it will be an excellent help for us in time. They found seven or eight Indian houses, but not lately inhabited. When they saw the houses they were in some fear, for they were but two persons and one piece.

Tuesday, the 9th of January, was a reasonable fair day, and we went to labor that day in the building of our town, in two rows of houses for more safety. We divided by lot the plot of ground whereon to build our town. After the proportion formerly allotted, we agreed that every man should build his own house, thinking by that course men would make more haste than working in common. The common house, in which for the first we made our rendezvous, being near finished wanted only covering, it being about twenty feet

---

[78] I.e., approximately 600 feet.

square. Some should make mortar, and some gather thatch, so that in four days half of it was thatched. Frost and foul weather hindered us much, this time of the year seldom could we work half the week.

Thursday, the 11th, William Bradford being at work (for it was a fair day) was vehemently taken with a grief and pain, and so shot to his huckle-bone.[79] It was doubted that he would have instantly died; he got cold in the former discoveries, especially the last, and felt some pain in his ankles by times, but he grew a little better towards night and in time, through God's mercy in the use of means, recovered.

Friday, the 12th, we went to work, but about noon it began to rain that it forced us to give over work.

This day two of our people put us in great sorrow and care; there was four sent to gather and cut thatch in the morning, and two of them, John Goodman and Peter Brown, having cut thatch all the forenoon, went to a further place, and willed the other two to bind up that which was cut and to follow them. So they did, being about a mile and a half from our plantation. But when the two came after, they could not find them, nor hear any thing of them at all, though they hallooed and shouted as loud as they could, so they returned to the company and told them of it. Whereupon Master Leaver[80] and three or four more went to seek them, but could hear nothing of them, so they returning, sent

---

[79] hip-bone

[80] Presumably a misprint for *Carver*. There is no other mention of a Leaver in the party.

more, but that night they could hear nothing at all of them. The next day they armed ten or twelve men out, verily thinking the Indians had surprised them. They went seeking seven or eight miles, but could neither see nor hear any thing at all, so they returned, with much discomfort to us all.

These two that were missed, at dinner time took their meat in their hands, and would go walk and refresh themselves. So going a little off they find a lake of water, and having a great mastiff bitch[81] with them and a spaniel, by the water side they found a great deer; the dogs chased him, and they followed so far as they lost themselves and could not find the way back. They wandered all that afternoon being wet, and at night it did freeze and snow. They were slenderly appareled and had no weapons but each one his sickle, nor any victuals. They ranged up and down and could find none of the savages' habitations. When it drew to night they were much perplexed, for they could find neither harbor nor meat, but, in frost and snow were forced to make the earth their bed and the element their covering. And another thing did very much terrify them; they heard, as they thought, two lions roaring exceedingly for a long time together, and a third, that they thought was very near them. So not knowing what to do, they resolved to climb up into a tree as their safest refuge, though that would prove an intolerable cold lodging; so they stood at the tree's root, that when the lions came they might take their

---

[81] dog

opportunity of climbing up. The bitch they were fain to hold by the neck, for she would have been gone to the lion; but it pleased God so to dispose, that the wild beasts came not. So they walked up and down under the tree all night; it was an extreme cold night. So soon as it was light they travelled again, passing by many lakes and brooks and woods, and in one place where the savages had burnt the space of five miles in length, which is a fine champaign[82] country, and even. In the afternoon, it pleased God, from a high hill they discovered the two isles in the bay, and so that night got to the plantation, being ready to faint with travail and want of victuals, and almost famished with cold. John Goodman was fain to have his shoes cut off his feet they were so swelled with cold, and it was a long while after ere he was able to go; those on the shore were much comforted at their return, but they on shipboard were grieved at deeming them lost.

---

[82] open

**Plymouth, Massachusetts - Authentic midcentury lithograph by
James F. Murray from 1930-1960**

But the next day, being the 14th of January, in the
morning about six of the clock the wind being very
great, they on shipboard spied their great new
rendezvous[83] on fire, which was to them a new
discomfort, fearing because of the supposed loss of the
men, that the savages had fired them. Neither could
they presently go to them, for want of water, but after
three quarters of an hour they went, as they had
purposed the day before to keep the Sabbath on shore,
because now there was the greater number of people.
At their landing they heard good tidings of the return
of the two men, and that the house was fired
occasionally by a spark that flew into the thatch,
which instantly burnt it all up but the roof stood and
little hurt. The most loss was Master Carver's and
William Bradford's, who then lay sick in bed, and if

---

[83] *village*

they had not risen with good speed, had been blown up with powder, but, through God's mercy, they had no harm. The house was as full of beds as they could lie one by another, and their muskets charged, but, blessed be God, there was no harm done.

Monday, the 15th day, it rained much all day, that they on shipboard could not go on shore, nor they on shore do any labor but were all wet.

Tuesday, Wednesday, Thursday, were very fair sunshiny days, as if it had been in April, and our people, so many as were in health, wrought cheerfully.

The 19th day we resolved to make a shed to put our common provision in, of which some were already set on shore, but at noon it rained, that we could not work. This day in the evening, John Goodman went abroad to use his lame feet, that were pitifully ill with the cold he had got, having a little spaniel with him. A little way from the plantation two great wolves ran after the dog; the dog ran to him and betwixt his legs for succor. He had nothing in his hand but took up a stick, and threw at one of them and hit him, and they presently ran both away, but came again; he got a pale-board[84] in his hand, and they sat both on their tails, grinning at him a good while, and went their way and left him.

---

[84] fence-stave

Saturday, 20th, we made up our shed for our common goods.

Sunday, the 21st, we kept our meeting[85] on land.

Monday, the 22nd, was a fair day. We wrought on our houses, and in the afternoon carried up our hogsheads of meal to our common storehouse. The rest of the week we followed our business likewise.

Monday, the 29th, in the morning cold frost and sleet, but after reasonable fair; both the long-boat and the shallop brought our common goods on shore.

Tuesday and Wednesday, 30th and 31st of January, cold frosty weather and sleet, that we could not work. In the morning the master and others saw two savages that had been on the island near our ship. What they came for we could not tell; they were going so far back again before they were descried, that we could not speak with them.

Sunday, the 4th of February, was very wet and rainy, with the greatest gusts of wind that ever we had since we came forth, that though we rid in a very good harbor, yet we were in danger, because our ship was light, the goods taken out, and she unballasted; and it caused much daubing[86] of our houses to fall down.

_____

[85] *church*

[86] This may refer to mud used for plastering the inner side of clapboard walls, typical of the frame houses which were among the first permanent buildings at Plymouth. During these early months, however, it may conceivably refer to a more fundamental structural

Friday, the 9th, still the cold weather continued, that we could do little work. That afternoon our little house for our sick people was set on fire by a spark that kindled in the roof, but no great harm was done. That evening, the master going ashore, killed five geese, which he friendly distributed among the sick people. He found also a good deer killed; the savages had cut off the horns, and a wolf was eating of him; how he came there we could not conceive.

Friday, the 16th, was a fair day, but the northerly wind continued, which continued the frost. This day after noon one of our people being a-fowling, and having taken a stand by a creek-side in the reeds, about a mile and a half from our plantation, there came by him twelve Indians marching towards our plantation, and in the woods he heard the noise of many more. He lay close till they were passed, and then with what speed he could he went home and gave the alarm, so the people abroad in the woods returned and armed themselves, but saw none of them; only toward the evening they made a great fire, about the place where they were first discovered. Captain Miles Standish and Francis Cook, being at work in the woods, coming home, left their tools behind them, but before they returned their tools were taken away by the savages. This coming of the savages gave us occasion to keep more strict watch, and to make our

feature in temporary huts of wattle-and-daub construction, where mud is the principal material, daubed over a framework of small saplings.

pieces and furniture ready, which by the moisture and rain were out of temper.

Saturday, the 17th day, in the morning we called a meeting for the establishing of military orders among ourselves, and we chose Miles Standish our captain[87], and gave him authority of command in affairs. And as we were in consultation hereabouts, two savages presented themselves upon the top of a hill, over against our plantation, about a quarter of a mile and less, and made signs unto us to come unto them; we likewise made signs unto them to come to us, whereupon we armed ourselves, and stood ready, and sent two over the brook towards them, to wit, Captain Standish and Stephen Hopkins, who went towards them. Only one of them had a musket, which they laid down on the ground in their sight, in sign of peace, and to parley with them, but the savages would not tarry their coming. A noise of a great many more was heard behind the hill, but no more came in sight. This caused us to plant our great ordnances[88] in places most convenient.

Wednesday, the 21st of February, the master came on shore with many of his sailors, and brought with him one of the great pieces, called a minion,[89] and helped us to draw it up the hill, with another piece that lay on

---

[87] *Read his complete story in Miles Standish: Puritan Captain, by Knowledge Keepers Bookstore, 2021.*

[88] *weapons*

[89] A cannon with 3¼ inch bore, firing a 4 pound shot.

shore, and mounted them, and a saller,[90] and two bases.[91] He brought with him a very fat goose to eat with us, and we had a fat crane, and a mallard, and a dried neat's[92] tongue, and so we were kindly and friendly together.

Saturday, the 3rd of March, the wind was south, the morning misty, but towards noon warm and fair weather; the birds sang in the woods most pleasantly. At one of the clock it thundered, which was the first we heard in that country; it was strong and great claps, but short, but after an hour it rained very sadly[93] till midnight.

Wednesday, the 7th of March, the wind was full east, cold, but fair. That day Master Carver with five others went to the great ponds, which seem to be excellent fishing-places; all the way they went they found it exceedingly beaten and haunted with deer, but they saw none. Amongst other fowl, they saw one a milk-white fowl, with a very black head. This day some garden seeds were sown.

Friday, the 16th, a fair warm day towards; this morning we determined to conclude of the military orders, which we had begun to consider of before but were interrupted by the savages, as we mentioned

---

[90] Presumably a misprint for *saker*, a cannon with 4 inch bore, firing a 6 pound shot.

[91] small cannons with 1¼ inch bore, firing ½ pound shot

[92] beef's

[93] hard; steadily

formerly. And whilst we were busied hereabout, we were interrupted again, for there presented himself a savage, which caused an alarm. He very boldly came all alone and along the houses straight to the rendezvous, where we intercepted him,[94] not suffering him to go in, as undoubtedly he would, out of his boldness. He saluted us in English, and bade us welcome, for he had learned some broken English among the Englishmen that came to fish at Monchiggon,[95] and knew by name the most of the captains, commanders, and masters that usually come. He was a man free in speech, so far as he could express his mind, and of a seemly carriage. We questioned him of many things; he was the first savage we could meet withal. He said he was not of these parts, but of Morattiggon, and one of the sagamores or lords thereof, and had been eight months in these parts, it lying hence a day's sail with a great wind, and five days by land. He discoursed of the whole country, and of every province, and of their sagamores, and their number of men, and strength. The wind beginning to rise a little, we cast a horseman's coat about him, for he was stark naked, only a leather about his waist, with a fringe about a span[96] long, or little more; he had a bow and two arrows, the one headed, and the other unheaded. He was a tall straight man, the hair of his head black, long behind,

---

[94] On first encounter, the Pilgrims were hardly hospitable to Samoset, whose friendly help in many respects was invaluable to them in later years.

[95] Presumably, Monhegan Island, off southeastern Maine.

[96] I.e., 9 inches.

only short before, none on his face at all; he asked some beer, but we gave him strong water[97] and biscuit, and butter, and cheese, and pudding, and a piece of mallard, all which he liked well, and had been acquainted with such amongst the English. He told us the place where we now live is called Patuxet, and that about four years ago all the inhabitants died of an extraordinary plague,[98] and there is neither man, woman, nor child remaining, as indeed we have found none, so as there is none to hinder our possession, or to lay claim unto it. All the afternoon we spent in communication with him; we would gladly have been rid of him at night, but he was not willing to go this night. Then we thought to carry him on shipboard, wherewith he was well content, and went into the shallop, but the wind was high and the water scant, that it could not return back. We lodged him that night at Stephen Hopkin's house, and watched him.

The next day he went away back to the Massasoits,[99] from whence he said he came, who are our next bordering neighbors. They are sixty strong, as he saith. The Nausets are as near southeast of them, and are a hundred strong, and those were they of whom our people were encountered, as we before related. They are much incensed and provoked against

---

[97] A generic term for liquor.

[98] The fact that bubonic plague had recently decimated a major portion of the indigenous population along the entire coast of New England was interpreted by the Pilgrims as divine intervention, and served as a convenient rationalization for English claims to the land.

[99] I.e., to the Wampanoag village where Massasoit was sachem.

the English, and about eight months ago slew three Englishmen, and two more hardly escaped by flight to Monchiggon; they were Sir Ferdinando Gorges his men,[100] as this savage told us, as he did likewise of the *huggery*, that is, fight, that our discoverers had with the Nausets, and of our tools that were taken out of the woods, which we willed him should be brought again, otherwise, we would right ourselves. These people are ill affected towards the English, by reason of one Hunt,[101] a master of a ship, who deceived the people, and got them under color of trucking[102] with them, twenty out of this very place where we inhabit, and seven men from the Nausets, and carried them away, and sold them for slaves[103] like a wretched man (for twenty pound a man) that cares not what mischief he doth for his profit.

Saturday, in the morning we dismissed the savage, and gave him a knife, a bracelet, and a ring; he promised within a night or two to come again, and to bring with him some of the Massasoits, our neighbors, with such beavers' skins as they had to truck with us.

Saturday and Sunday, reasonable fair days. On this day came again the savage, and brought with him five other tall proper men; they had every man a deer's

---

[100] Actually members of a crew led by Capt. Thomas Dermer, on an expedition sponsored by Gorges. (*See Valiant Navigators by Knowledge Keepers Bookstore.*)

[101] Thomas Hunt, captain of a ship in Capt. John Smith's company.

[102] *trading*

[103] (in Spain)

skin on him, and the principal of them had a wild cat's skin, or such like on the one arm. They had most of them long hosen[104] up to their groins, close made; and above their groins to their waist another leather, they were altogether like the Irish-trousers.[105] They are of complexion like our English gypsies, no hair or very little on their faces, on their heads long hair to their shoulders, only cut before[106], some trussed up before with a feather, broad-wise, like a fan, another a fox tail hanging out. These left (according to our charge given him before) their bows and arrows a quarter of a mile from our town. We gave them entertainment as we thought was fitting them; they did eat liberally of our English victuals. They made semblance unto us of friendship and amity; they sang and danced after their manner, like antics.[107] They brought with them in a thing like a bow-case (which the principal of them had about his waist) a little of their corn pounded to powder, which, put to a little water, they eat. He had a little tobacco in a bag, but none of them drank[108] but when he listed[109]. Some of them had their faces painted black, from the forehead to the chin, four or five fingers broad; others after other fashions, as they liked. They brought three or four skins, but we would not truck with them at all that day, but wished them

---

[104] leggings

[105] Ireland was little better known than New England in the early seventeenth century, and comparisons between Indians and Irishmen are frequent in the descriptive accounts of English explorers of the period.

[106] *In front*

[107] clowns

[108] smoked

[109] *Or, wanted to*

to bring more, and we would truck for all, which they promised within a night or two, and would leave these behind them, though we were not willing they should, and they brought us all our tools again which were taken in the woods, in our men's absence. So because of the day we dismissed them so soon as we could. But Samoset, our first acquaintance, either was sick, or feigned himself so, and would not go with them, and stayed with us till Wednesday morning. Then we sent him to them, to know the reason they came not according to their words, and we gave him a hat, a pair of stockings and shoes, a shirt, and a piece of cloth to tie about his waist.

The Sabbath day, when we sent them from us, we gave every one of them some trifles, especially the principal of them. We carried them along with our arms to the place where they left their bows and arrows, whereat they were amazed, and two of them began to slink away, but that the other called them. When they took their arrows, we bade them farewell, and they were glad, and so with many thanks given us they departed, with promise they would come again.

Monday and Tuesday proved fair days; we digged our grounds, and sowed our garden seeds.

Wednesday a fine warm day, we sent away Samoset.

That day we had again a meeting to conclude of laws and orders for ourselves, and to confirm those military orders that were formerly propounded and twice broken off by the savages' coming, but so we were again the third time, for after we had been an hour together on the top of the hill over against us two or three savages presented themselves, that made semblance of daring us, as we thought. So Captain Standish with another, with their muskets went over to them, with two of the master's mates that follow them without arms, having two muskets with them. They whetted and rubbed their arrows and strings, and made show of defiance, but when our men drew near them, they ran away; thus were we again interrupted by them. This day with much ado we got our carpenter that had been long sick of the scurvy, to fit our shallop, to fetch all from aboard.

Thursday, the 22nd of March, was a very fair warm day. About noon we met again about our public business, but we had scarce been an hour together, but Samoset came again, and Squanto, the only native of Patuxet, (where we now inhabit, who was one of the twenty captives that by Hunt were carried away, and had been in England,[110] and dwelt in Cornhill with Master John Slanie, a merchant, and could speak a little English), with three others, and they brought with them some few skins to truck, and some red herrings newly taken and dried, but not salted, and signified unto us, that their great sagamore Massasoit was hard by, with Quadequina his brother, and all their men. They could not well express in English

---

[110] The adventures of Samoset, Squanto, and other Indians who had been kidnapped and taken to Europe before whites settled in New England are recounted with accuracy and appropriate color by Carolyn T. Foreman, *Indians Abroad*, 1493-1938 (Norman, 1943).

what they would, but after an hour the king came to the top of a hill over against us, and had in his train sixty men, that we could well behold them and they us. We were not willing to send our governor to them, and they unwilling to come to us, so Squanto went again unto him, who brought word that we should send one to parley with him, which we did, which was Edward Winslow, to know his mind, and to signify the mind and will of our governor, which was to have trading and peace with him. We sent to the king a pair of knives, and a copper chain with a jewel at it. To Quadequina we sent likewise a knife and a jewel to hang in his ear, and withal a pot of strong water, a good quantity of biscuit, and some butter, which were all willingly accepted.

Our messenger made a speech unto him, that King James saluted him with words of love and peace, and did accept of him as his friend and ally, and that our governor desired to see him and to truck with him, and to confirm a peace with him, as his next neighbor. He liked well of the speech and heard it attentively, though the interpreters did not well express it. After he had eaten and drunk himself, and given the rest to his company, he looked upon our messenger's sword and armor which he had on, with intimation of his desire to buy it, but on the other side, our messenger showed his unwillingness to part with it. In the end he left him in the custody of Quadequina his brother, and came over the brook, and some twenty men following him, leaving all their bows and arrows behind them. We kept six or seven as hostages for our messenger;

Captain Standish and Master Williamson[111] met the king at the brook, with half a dozen musketeers. They saluted him and he them, so one going over, the one on the one side, and the other on the other, conducted him to a house then in building, where we placed a green rug and three or four cushions. Then instantly came our governor with drum and trumpet after him, and some few musketeers. After salutations, our governor kissing his hand, the king kissed him, and so they sat down. The governor called for some strong water, and drunk to him, and he drunk a great draught that made him sweat all the while after; he called for a little fresh meat, which the king did eat willingly, and did give his followers. Then they treated of peace, which was:

The agreements of peace between us and Massasoit.

1. That neither he nor any of his should injure or do hurt to any of our people.

2. And if any of his did hurt to any of ours, he should send the offender, that we might punish him.

3. That if any of our tools were taken away when our people were at work, he should cause them

---

[111] Presumably a misprint for *Williams*. There is no other mention of a Williamson in the early Plymouth sources.

to be restored, and if ours did any harm to any of his, we would do the like to them.

4. If any did unjustly war against him, we would aid him; if any did war against us, he should aid us.

5. He should send to his neighbor confederates, to certify them of this, that they might not wrong us, but might be likewise comprised in the conditions of peace.

6. That when their men came to us, they should leave their bows and arrows behind them, as we should do our pieces when we came to them.

Lastly, that doing thus, King James would esteem of him as his friend and ally.

All which the king seemed to like well,[112] and it was applauded of his followers; all the while he sat by the governor he trembled for fear. In his person he is a very lusty man, in his best years, an able body, grave of countenance, and spare of speech. In his attire little or nothing differing from the rest of his followers, only in a great chain of white bone beads about his neck, and at it behind his neck hangs a little bag of tobacco, which he drank and gave us to drink; his face was

---

[112] This first American mutual security pact remained inviolate throughout Massasoit's life. He and his eldest son Wamsutta (named "Alexander" by the English) signed such a treaty in Plymouth in 1639, and it was ratified and confirmed by the colonial government. The peace was broken in 1675, for which most historians blame Wamsutta's brother and successor, Metacom ("King Philip").

painted with a sad[113] red like murry,[114] and oiled both head and face, that he looked greasily. All his followers likewise, were in their faces, in part or in whole painted, some black, some red, some yellow, and some white, some with crosses, and other antic works; some had skins on them, and some naked, all strong, tall, all men in appearance.

So after all was done, the governor conducted him to the brook, and there they embraced each other and he departed; we diligently keeping our hostages, we expected our messenger's coming, but anon, word was brought us that Quadequina was coming, and our messenger was stayed till his return, who presently came and a troop with him, so likewise we entertained him, and conveyed him to the place prepared. He was very fearful of our pieces, and made signs of dislike, that they should be carried away, whereupon commandment was given they should be laid away. He was a very proper tall young man, of a very modest and seemly countenance, and he did kindly like of our entertainment, so we conveyed him likewise as we did the king, but divers of their people stayed still. When he was returned, then they dismissed our messenger. Two of his people would have stayed all night, but we would not suffer it. One thing I forgot, the king had in his bosom, hanging in a string, a great long knife; he marvelled much at our trumpet, and some of his men would sound it as well as they could. Samoset and

---

[113] deep
[114] mulberry

Squanto, they stayed all night with us, and the king and all his men lay all night in the woods, not above half an English mile from us, and all their wives and women with them. They said that within eight or nine days they would come and set corn on the other side of the brook, and dwell there all summer, which is hard by us. That night we kept good watch, but there was no appearance of danger.

The next morning divers of their people came over to us, hoping to get some victuals as we imagined; some of them told us the king would have some of us come see him. Captain Standish and Isaac Allerton went venturously, who were welcomed of him after their manner: he gave them three or four ground-nuts, and some tobacco. We cannot yet conceive but that he is willing to have peace with us, for they have seen our people sometimes alone two or three in the woods at work and fowling, when as they offered them no harm as they might easily have done, and especially because he hath a potent adversary the Narragansets, that are at war with him, against whom he thinks we may be some strength to him, for our pieces[115] are terrible unto them. This morning they stayed till ten or eleven of the clock, and our governor bid them send the king's kettle, and filled it full of pease[116], which pleased them well, and so they went their way.

Friday was a very fair day; Samoset and Squanto still remained with us. Squanto went at noon to fish for eels; at night he came home with as many as he could well lift in one hand, which our people were glad of. They were fat and sweet; he trod them out with his feet, and so caught them with his hands without any other instrument.

This day we proceeded on with our common business, from which we had been so often hindered by the savages' coming, and concluding both of military orders and of some laws and orders as we thought behooveful for our present estate, and condition, and did likewise choose our governor for this year, which was Master John Carver, a man well approved amongst us.

---

[115] *weapons*
[116] *peas*

A Journey to Pokanoket, the habitation of the great King Massasoit; as also our message, the answer and entertainment we had of him.

It seemed good to the company for many considerations to send some amongst them to Massasoit, the greatest commander amongst the savages bordering upon us; partly to know where to find them if occasion served, as also to see their strength, discover the country, prevent abuses in their disorderly coming unto us, make satisfaction for some conceived injuries to be done on our parts, and to continue the league of peace and friendship between them and us. For these, and the like ends, it pleased the governor to make choice of Stephen Hopkins and Edward Winslow to go unto him, and having a fit opportunity,[117] by reason of a savage called Squanto (that could speak English) coming unto us, with all expedition provided a horseman's coat of red cotton, and laced with a slight lace, for a present, that both they and their message might be the more acceptable amongst them.

The message was as followeth: that forasmuch as his subjects came often and without fear, upon all occasions amongst us, so we were now come unto him, and in witness of the love and good-will the English bear unto him, the governor hath sent him a coat,

---

[117] The journey to Pokanoket took place in the summer of 1621. During the preceding three months, which are unreported in this journal, Bradford notes that almost half of the settlers died in the "General Sickness." None abandoned the enterprise, however, and the *Mayflower* returned empty to England.

desiring that the peace and amity that was between them and us might be continued, not that we feared them, but because we intended not to injure any, desiring to live peaceably, and as with all men, so especially with them, our nearest neighbors.

But whereas his people came very often, and very many together unto us, bringing for the most part their wives and children with them, they were welcome; yet we being but strangers as yet at Patuxet, alias *New Plymouth*,[118] and not knowing how our corn might prosper, we could no longer give them such entertainment as we had done, and as we desired still to do. Yet if he would be pleased to come himself, or any special friend of his desired to see us, coming from him they should be welcome; and to the end we might know them from others, our governor had sent him a copper chain, desiring if any messenger should come from him to us, we might know him by bringing it with him, and hearken and give credit to his message accordingly. Also requesting him that such as have skins should bring them to us, and that he would hinder the multitude from oppressing us with them.

---

[118] The derivation of this name is not clear. Six different spellings occur even within this book: *Plimoth, and New Plimoth* (both on the title page!), *Plimouth, Plimmouth, New Plimmouth*, and *New Plimmouth*. It is true that Plymouth was the town from which the settlers had finally set sail from their native country, "... having been kindly entertained and courteously used by divers friends there dwelling." Furthermore, the land company which granted their patent had once been called the Plymouth Company. But we need evoke neither sentimentalism nor commercial diplomacy on the part of the Pilgrims to account for the name. In fact, this site was called "Plimouth" on the map which they carried on the *Mayflower*, from Capt. John Smith's *Description of New England* (London, 1616); supposedly it was arbitrarily so designated by Prince Charles when Smith showed him a draft of the map.

And whereas at our first arrival at Paomet (called by us Cape Cod) we found there corn buried in the ground, and finding no inhabitants but some graves of dead new buried, took the corn, resolving if ever we could hear of any that had right thereunto, to make satisfaction to the full for it, yet since we understand the owners thereof were fled for fear of us, our desire was either to pay them with the like quantity of corn, English meal, or any other commodities we had to pleasure them withal; requesting him that some one of his men might signify so much unto them, and we would content him for his pains. And last of all, our governor requested one favor of him, which was, that he would exchange some of their corn for seed with us, that we might make trial which best agreed with the soil where we live.

With these presents and message we set forward the 10th June, about nine o'clock in the morning, our guide resolving that night to rest at Nemasket,[119] a town under Massasoit, and conceived by us to be very near, because the inhabitants flocked so thick upon every slight occasion amongst us; but we found it to be some fifteen English miles. On the way we found some ten or twelve men, women, and children, which had pestered us till we were weary of them, perceiving that (as the manner of them all is) where victual is easiest to be got, there they live, especially in the summer: by reason whereof, our bay affording many lobsters, they

---

[119] Now, Middleborough, Massachusetts.

resort every spring-tide thither; and now returned with us to Nemasket.

Thither we came about three o'clock after noon, the inhabitants entertaining us with joy, in the best manner they could, giving us a kind of bread called by them *maizium*, and the spawn of shads, which then they got in abundance, insomuch as they gave us spoons to eat them. With these they boiled musty acorns, but of the shads we ate heartily. After this they desired one of our men to shoot at a crow, complaining what damage they sustained in their corn by them, who shooting some fourscore off and killing, they much admired it, as other shots on other occasions.

After this, Squanto told us we should hardly in one day reach Pokanoket,[120] moving us to go some eight miles further, where we should find more store and better victuals than there. Being willing to hasten our journey we went, and came thither at sunsetting, where we found many of the Namascheucks (they so calling the men of Nemasket) fishing upon a weir which they had made on a river which belonged to them, where they caught abundance of bass. These welcomed us also, gave us of their fish, and we them of our victuals, not doubting but we should have enough where'er we came. There we lodged in the open fields, for houses they had none, though they spent the most of the summer there. The head of this river is reported

---

[120] Now, the Mount Hope area of Bristol, Rhode Island.

to be not far from the place of our abode; upon it are and have been many towns, it being a good length. The ground is very good on both sides, it being for the most part cleared. Thousands of men have lived there, which died in a great plague not long since; and pity it was and is to see so many goodly fields, and so well seated, without men to dress and manure[121] the same. Upon this river dwelleth Massasoit. It cometh into the sea at the Narraganset Bay, where the Frenchmen so much use. A ship may go many miles up it, as the savages report, and a shallop to the head of it; but so far as we saw, we are sure a shallop may.

But to return to our journey. The next morning we broke our fast, took our leave and departed, being then accompanied with some six savages. Having gone about six miles by the river side, at a known shoal place, it being low water, they spake to us to put off our breeches, for we must wade through. Here let me not forget the valor and courage of some of the savages on the opposite side of the river, for there were remaining alive only two men, both aged, especially the one being above threescore. These two, espying a company of men entering the river, ran very swiftly and low in the grass, to meet us at the bank, where with shrill voices and great courage standing charged upon us with their bows; they demanded what we were, supposing us to be enemies, and thinking to take advantage on us in the water. But seeing we were

---

[121] cultivate; till

113

friends, they welcomed us with such food as they had, and we bestowed a small bracelet of beads on them. Thus far we are sure the tide ebbs and flows.

Having here again refreshed ourselves we proceeded in our journey, the weather being very hot for travel, yet the country so well watered that a man could scarce be dry, but he should have a spring at hand to cool his thirst, beside small rivers in abundance. But the savages will not willingly drink but at a springhead. When we came to any small brook where no bridge was, two of them desired to carry us through of their own accords, also fearing we were or would be weary, offered to carry our pieces, also if we would lay off any of our clothes, we should have them carried; and as the one of them had found more special kindness from one of the messengers, and the other savage from the other so they showed their thankfulness accordingly in affording us all help and furtherance in the journey.

As we passed along, we observed that there were few places by the river but had been inhabited, by reason whereof much ground was clear, save of weeds which grew higher than our heads. There is much good timber, both oak, walnut tree, fir, beech, and exceeding great chestnut trees. The country, in respect of the lying of it, is both champaign and hilly, like many places in England. In some places it is very rocky both above ground and in it. And though the country be wild and overgrown with woods, yet the trees stand not thick, but a man may well ride a horse amongst them.

Passing on at length, one of the company, an Indian, espied a man and told the rest of it. We asked them if they feared any; they told us that if they were Narraganset men they would not trust them. Whereat we called for our pieces and bid them not to fear, for though they were twenty, we two alone would not care for[122] them. But they hailing him, he proved a friend, and had only two women with him; their baskets were empty but they fetched water in their bottles, so that we drank with them and departed. After, we met another man with other two women, which had been at rendezvous by the salt water, and their baskets were full of roasted crab, fishes, and other dried shell fish, of which they gave us, and we ate and drank with them, and gave each of the women a string of beads, and departed.

After, we came to a town of Massasoit's, where we ate oysters and other fish. From thence we went to Pokanoket but Massasoit was not at home; there we stayed, he being sent for. When news was brought of his coming, our guide Squanto requested that at our meeting we would discharge our pieces. But one of us going about to charge his piece, the women and children, through fear to see him take up his piece, ran away, and could not be pacified till he laid it down

---

[122] *fear*

again, who afterward were better informed by our interpreter.

Massasoit being come, we discharged our pieces, and saluted him, who after their manner kindly welcomed us, and took us into his house, and set us down by him, where, having delivered our foresaid message and presents, and having put the coat on his back and the chain about his neck, he was not a little proud to behold himself, and his men also to see their king so bravely[123] attired.

For answer to our message, he told us we were welcome, and he would gladly continue that peace and friendship which was between him and us, and, for his men, they should no more pester us as they had done; also that he would sent to Paomet, and would help us with corn for seed, according to our request.

This being done, his men gathered near to him, to whom he turned himself, and made a great speech; they sometimes interposing, and, as it were, confirming and applauding him in that he said. The meaning whereof was (as far as we could learn) thus: Was not he Massasoit, commander of the country about them? Was not such a town his, and the people of it? And should they not bring their skins unto us? To which they answered, they were his and would be at peace with us, and bring their skins to us. After this manner he named at least thirty places, and their

---

[123] admirably

answer was as aforesaid to every one, so that as it was delightful, it was tedious unto us.

This being ended, he lighted tobacco for us, and fell to discoursing of England, and of the King's Majesty, marvelling that he would live without a wife.[124] Also he talked of the Frenchmen, bidding us not to suffer them to come to Narraganset, for it was King James his country, and he also was King James his man. Late it grew, but victuals he offered none, for indeed he had not any, being he came so newly home. So we desired to go to rest. He laid us on the bed with himself and his wife, they at the one end and we at the other, it being only planks laid a foot from the ground, and a thin mat upon them. Two more of his chief men,

---

[124] The wife of James I had died more than a year before the Pilgrims sailed from England.

117

for want of room, pressed by and upon us, so that we were worse weary of our lodging than of our journey.

The next day, being Thursday, many of their sachems, or petty governors, came to see us, and many of their men also. There they went to their manner of games for skins and knives. There we challenged them to shoot with them for skins, but they durst not; only they desired to see one of us shoot at a mark, who shooting with hail-shot, they wondered to see the mark so full of holes.

About one o'clock, Massasoit brought two fishes that he had shot; they were like bream but three times so big, and better meat. These being boiled there were at least forty looked for share in them, the most ate of them. This meal only we had in two nights and a day, and had not one of us bought a partridge, we had taken our journey fasting. Very importunate he was to have us stay with them longer. But we desired to keep the Sabbath at home, and feared we should either be light-headed for want of sleep, for what with bad lodging, the savages' barbarous singing (for they use to sing themselves asleep), lice and fleas within doors, and mosquitoes without, we could hardly sleep all the time of our being there; we much fearing that if we should stay any longer, we should not be able to recover home for want of strength. So that on the Friday morning before sunrising, we took our leave and departed, Massasoit being both grieved and ashamed that he could no better entertain us, and retaining Squanto to send from place to place to procure truck for us, and appointing another, called Tokamahamon, in his place, whom we had found faithful before and after upon all occasions.

At this town of Massasoit's where we before ate, we were again refreshed with a little fish, and bought about a handful of meal of their parched corn, which was very precious at that time of the year, and a small string of dried shell-fish, as big as oysters. The latter we gave to the six savages that accompanied us, keeping the meal for ourselves. When we drank, we ate each a spoonful of it with a pipe of tobacco, instead of other victuals, and of this also we could not but give them so long as it lasted. Five miles they led us to a house out of the way in hope of victuals, but we found nobody there and so were but worse able to return home. That night we reached to the weir where we lay before, but the Namascheucks were returned, so that we had no hope of any thing there. One of the savages had shot a shad in the water, and a small squirrel as big as a rat, called a *neuxis*; the one half of either he gave us, and after went to the weir to fish. From hence we wrote to Plymouth, and sent Tokamahamon before to Nemasket, willing him from thence to send another, that he might meet us with food at Nemasket. Two men now only remained with us, and it pleased God to give them good store of fish, so that we were well refreshed. After supper we went to rest, and they to fishing again; more they got and fell to eating afresh, and retained sufficient ready roast for all our breakfasts. About two o'clock in the morning arose a great storm of wind, rain, lightning, and thunder, in such violent manner that we could not keep in our fire, and had the savages not roasted fish when we were asleep, we had set forward fasting, for the rain still continued with great violence, even the whole day through, till we came within two miles of home.

Being wet and weary, at length we came to Nemasket; there we refreshed ourselves, giving gifts to all such as had showed us any kindness. Amongst others, one of the six that came with us from Pokanoket, having before this on the way unkindly forsaken us, marveled we gave him nothing, and told us what he had done for us. We also told him of some discourtesies he offered us, whereby he deserved nothing. Yet we gave him a small trifle, whereupon he offered us tobacco; but the house being full of people, we told them he stole some by the way, and if it were of that we would not take it, for we would not receive that which was stolen upon any terms; if we did, our God would be angry with us, and destroy us. This abashed him and gave the rest great content. But at our departure he would needs carry him on his back through a river, whom he had formerly in some sort abused. Fain they would have had us to lodge there all night, and wondered we would set forth again in such weather. But, God be praised, we came safe home that night, though wet, weary, and surbated.[125]

---

[125] fatigued; bruised

A voyage made by ten of our men to the Kingdom of Nauset, to seek a boy that had lost himself in the woods; with such accidents as befell us in that voyage.

The 11th of June we set forth, the weather being very fair. But ere we had been long at sea, there arose a storm of wind and rain, with much lightning and thunder, insomuch that a spout[126] arose not far from us, but, God be praised, it dured[127] not long, and we put in that night for harbor at a place called Cummaquid,[128] where we had some hope to find the boy. Two savages were in the boat with us, the one was Squanto, our interpreter, the other Tokamahamon, a special friend. It being night before we came in, we anchored in the midst of the bay, where we were dry at alow water. In the morning we espied savages seeking lobsters, and sent our two interpreters to speak with them, the channel being between them; where they told them what we were, and for what we were come, willing them not at all to fear us, for we would not hurt them. Their answer was, that the boy was well, but he was at Nauset;[129] yet since we were there they desired us to come ashore and eat with them; which, as soon as our boat floated, we did, and went six ashore, having four pledges for them in the boat. They brought us to their

---

[126] *tornado*
[127] endured
[128] Now, Barnstable, Massachusetts.
[129] Now, Eastham, Massachusetts.

sachem or governor, whom they call Iyanough, a man not exceeding twenty-six years of age, but very personable, gentle, courteous, and fair conditioned, indeed not like a savage, save for his attire. His entertainment was answerable to his parts, and his cheer plentiful and various.

One thing was very grievous unto us at this place. There was an old woman, whom we judged to be no less than a hundred years old, which came to see us because she never saw English, yet could not behold us without breaking forth into great passion, weeping and crying excessively. We demanding the reason of it, they told us she had three sons who, when Master Hunt was in these parts, went aboard his ship to trade with him, and he carried them captives into Spain (for Squanto at that time was carried away also) by which means she was deprived of the comfort of her children in her old age. We told them we were sorry that any Englishman should give them that offense, that Hunt was a bad man, and that all the English that heard of it condemned him for the same; but for us, we would not offer them any such injury though it would gain us all the skins in the country. So we gave her some small trifles, which somewhat appeased her.

After dinner we took boat for Nauset, Iyanough and two of his men accompanying us. Ere we came to Nauset, the day and tide were almost spent, insomuch as we could not go in with our shallop, but the sachem or governor of Cummaquid went ashore and his men with him. We also sent Squanto to tell Aspinet, the sachem of Nauset, wherefore we came. The savages here came very thick amongst us, and were earnest with us to bring in our boat. But we neither well could, nor yet desired to do it, because we had least cause to trust them, being they only had formerly made an assault upon us in the same place, in time of our winter discovery for habitation. And indeed it was no marvel they did so, for howsoever, through snow or otherwise, we saw no houses, yet we were in the midst of them.

When our boat was aground they came very thick, but we stood therein upon our guard, not suffering any to enter except two, the one being of Manomoyik,[130] and one of those whose corn we had formerly found; we promised him restitution, and desired him either to come to Patuxet for satisfaction, or else we would bring them so much corn again. He promised to come; we used him very kindly for the present. Some few skins we got there but not many.

After sunset, Aspinet came with a great train, and brought the boy with him, one bearing him through the water. He had not less than a hundred with him, the half whereof came to the shallop side unarmed with him, the other stood aloof with their bows and arrows. There he delivered us the boy, behung with beads, and made peace with us, we bestowing a knife on him, and likewise on another that first entertained

---

[130] Now, Chatham, Massachusetts.

the boy and brought him thither. So they departed from us.

Here we understood that the Narragansets had spoiled[131] some of Massasoit's men, and taken him. This struck some fear in us, because the colony was so weakly guarded, the strength thereof being abroad. But we set forth with resolution to make the best haste home we could; yet the wind being contrary, having scarce any fresh water left, and at least sixteen leagues home, we put in again for the shore. There we met again with Iyanough, the sachem of Cummaquid, and the most of his town, both men, women, and children with him. He, being still willing to gratify us, took a runlet[132] and led our men in the dark a great way for water, but could find none good, yet brought such as there was on his neck with him. In the meantime the women joined hand in hand, singing and dancing before the shallop, the men also showing all the kindness they could, Iyanough himself taking a bracelet from about his neck and hanging it upon one of us.

Again we set out, but to small purpose, for we gat but little homeward.

Our water also was very brackish, and not to be drunk. The next morning, Iyanough espied us again and ran after us; we, being resolved to go to

---

[131] In early seventeenth-century usage, this could imply anything from disarming to kidnapping, from robbing to killing.

[132] small keg

Cummaquid again to water, took him into the shallop, whose entertainment was not inferior unto the former.

The soil at Nauset and here is alike, even and sandy, not so good for corn as where we are. Ships may safely ride in either harbor. In the summer they abound with fish. Being now watered we put forth again, and, by God's providence, came safely home that night.

**A journey to the Kingdom of Nemasket
in defense of the great King Massasoit, against
the Narragansets, and to revenge the supposed
death of our interpreter Squanto.**

At our return from Nauset, we found it true that
Massasoit was put from his country by the
Narragansets. Word also was brought unto us that
Corbitant, a petty sachem or governor under
Massasoit (whom they ever feared to be too conversant
with the Narragansets), was at Nemasket, who sought
to draw the hearts of Massasoit's subjects from him,
speaking also disdainfully of us, storming at the peace
between Nauset, Cummaquid, and us, and at Squanto,
the worker of it; also at Tokamahamon, and one
Hobomok (two Indians, or Lemes,[133] one of which he
would treacherously have murdered a little before,
being a special and trusty man of Massasoit's).
Tokamahamon went to him, but the other two would
not, yet put their lives in their hands, privately went
to see if they could hear of their king, and lodging at
Nemasket were discovered to Corbitant, who set a
guard to beset the house, and took Squanto (for he had
said, if he were dead the English had lost their
tongue). Hobomok, seeing that Squanto was taken,
and Corbitant held a knife at his breast, being a strong
and stout man, broke from them and came to New

---

[133] This passage defies interpretation. "Or Lemes" has no sense in seventeenth-century
English or local Indian languages. Most previous editors have assumed this to be a
misprint for *our allies*; I am not altogether happy with that interpretation but have
nothing better to offer.

Plymouth, full of fear and sorrow for Squanto, whom he thought to be slain.

Upon this news the company assembled together, and resolved on the morrow to send ten men armed to Nemasket, and Hobomok for their guide, to revenge the supposed death of Squanto on Corbitant our bitter enemy, and to retain Nepeof, another sachem or governor, who was of this confederacy, till we heard what was become of our friend Massasoit.

On the morrow we set out ten men armed, who took their journey as aforesaid, but the day proved very wet. When we supposed we were within three or four miles of Nemasket, we went out of the way and stayed there till night, because we would not be discovered. There we consulted what to do, and thinking best to beset the house at midnight, each was appointed his task by the captain, all men encouraging one another to the utmost of their power. By night our guide lost his way, which much discouraged our men, being we were wet, and weary of our arms, but one of our men, having been before at Nemasket, brought us into the way again.

Before we came to the town, we sat down and ate such as our knapsacks afforded. That being done, we threw them aside, and all such things as might hinder us, and so went on and beset the house, according to our last resolution. Those that entered demanded if Corbitant were not there, but fear had bereft the savages of speech. We charged them not to stir, for if

Corbitant were not there, we would not meddle with them; if he were, we came principally for him, to be avenged on him for the supposed death of Squanto, and other matters; but, howsoever, we would not at all hurt their women or children. Notwithstanding, some of them pressed out at a private door and escaped, but with some wounds. At length perceiving our principal ends, they told us Corbitant was returned with all his train, and that Squanto was yet living, and in the town, offering some tobacco, other such as they had to eat. In this hurly-burly we discharged two pieces at random, which much terrified all the inhabitants, except Squanto and Tokamahamon, who, though they knew not our end in coming, yet assured them of our honesty, that we would not hurt them. Those boys that were in the house, seeing our care of women, often cried, "*Neen squaes*," that is to say, "I am a woman"; the women also hanging upon Hobomok, calling him *Towam*, that is, "friend." But to be short, we kept them we had, and made them make a fire that we might see to search the house. In the meantime Hobomok got on the top of the house and called Squanto and Tokamahamon, which came unto us accompanied with others, some armed and others naked. Those that had bows and arrows, we took them away, promising them again when it was day. The house we took for our better safeguard, but released those we had taken, manifesting whom we came for and wherefore.

On the next morning we marched into the midst of the town, and went to the house of Squanto to breakfast.

Thither came all whose hearts were upright towards us, but all Corbitant's faction were fled away. There in the midst of them we manifested again our intendment, assuring them, that although Corbitant had now escaped us, yet there was no place should secure him and his from us if he continued his threatening us and provoking others against us, who had kindly entertained him, and never intended evil towards him till he now so justly deserved it. Moreover, if Massasoit did not return in safety from Narraganset, or if hereafter he should make any insurrection against him, or offer violence to Squanto, Hobomok, or any of Massasoit's subjects, we would revenge it upon him, to the overthrow of him and his. As for those were wounded, we were sorry for it, though themselves procured it in not staying in the house at our command; yet if they would return home with us, our surgeon should heal them.

At this offer, one man and a woman that were wounded went home with us, Squanto and many other known friends accompanying us, and offering all help that might be by carriage of any thing we had to ease us. So that, by God's good providence, we safely returned home the morrow night after we set forth.

A relation of our Voyage to the Massachusetts, and what happened there.

It seemed good to the company in general, that though the Massachusetts had often threatened us (as we were informed), yet we should go amongst them, partly to see the country, partly to make peace with them, and partly to procure their truck. For these ends the governors chose ten men fit for the purpose, and sent Squanto and two other savages to bring us to speech with the people, and interpret for us.

We set out about midnight,[134] the tide then serving for us. We supposing it to be nearer than it is, thought to be there the next morning betimes, but it proved well near twenty leagues[135] from New Plymouth.

We came into the bottom of the bay,[136] but being late we anchored and lay in the shallop, not having seen any of the people. The next morning we put in for the shore. There we found many lobsters that had been gathered together by the savages, which we made ready under a cliff. The captain set two sentinels behind the cliff to the landward to secure the shallop, and taking a guide with him and four of our company, went to seek the inhabitants; where they met a woman

---

[134] Bradford's *Of Plymouth Plantation* sets the date of this embarkation as 18 September 1621.
[135] *Sixty miles*
[136] I. e., Boston Harbor.

coming for her lobsters, they told her of them, and contented her for them. She told them where the people were. Squanto went to them; the rest returned, having direction which way to bring the shallop to them.

The sachem or governor of this place, is called Obbatinewat, and though he lives in the bottom of the Massachusetts Bay, yet he is under Massasoit. He used[137] us very kindly; he told us he durst not then remain in any settled place, for fear of the Tarentines.[138] Also the Squaw Sachem,[139] or Massachusetts' queen, was an enemy to him.

We told him of divers sachems that had acknowledged themselves to be King James his men, and if he also would submit himself, we would be his safeguard from his enemies, which he did, and went along with us to bring us to the Squaw Sachem. Again we crossed the bay, which is very large and hath at least fifty islands in it, but the certain number is not known to the inhabitants. Night it was before we came to that side of the bay where this people were. On shore the savages went but found nobody. That night also we rid[140] at anchor aboard the shallop.

On the morrow we went ashore, all but two men, and marched in arms up in the country. Having gone three

---

[137] *treated*

[138] Presumably, the Abnaki, an Algonquian tribe of eastern Maine.

[139] Presumably, the widow of Nanepashemet.

[140] *rode*

miles we came to a place where corn had been newly gathered, a house pulled down, and the people gone. A mile from hence, Nanepashemet, their king, in his lifetime had lived. His house was not like others, but a scaffold was largely built, with poles and planks some six feet from ground, and the house upon that, being situated on the top of a hill.

Not far from hence, in a bottom, we came to a fort built by their deceased king, the manner thus: there were poles some thirty or forty feet long, stuck in the ground as thick as they could be set one by another, and with these they enclosed a ring some forty of fifty feet over. A trench breast high was digged on each side; one way there was to go into it with a bridge; in the midst of this palisade stood the frame of a house wherein, being dead, he lay buried.

About a mile from hence, we came to such another, but seated on the top of a hill; here Nanepashemet was killed, none dwelling in it since the time of his death. At this place we stayed, and sent two savages to look the inhabitants, and to inform them of our ends in coming, that they might not be fearful of us. Within a mile of this place they found the women of the place together, with their corn on heaps, whither we supposed them to be fled for fear of us, and the more, because in divers places they had newly pulled down their houses, and for haste in one place had left some of their corn covered with a mat, and nobody with it.

With much fear they entertained us at first, but seeing our gentle carriage towards them, they took heart and entertained us in the best manner they could, boiling cod and such other things as they had for us. At length, with much sending for, came one of their men, shaking and trembling for fear. But when he saw we intended them no hurt, but came to truck, he promised us his skins also. Of him we inquired for their queen, but it seemed she was far from thence—at least we could not see her.

Here Squanto would have had us rifle the savage women, and taken their skins and all such things as might be serviceable for us; for (said he) they are a bad people, and have oft threatened you. But our answer was: Were they never so bad, we would not wrong them, or give them any just occasion against us; for their words, we little weighed them, but if they once attempted any thing against us, then we would deal far worse than he desired.

Having well spent the day, we returned to the shallop, almost all the women accompanying us to truck, who sold their coats from their backs, and tied boughs about them, but with great shamefacedness (for indeed they are more modest than some of our English women are). We promised them to come again to them, and they us, to keep their skins.

Within this bay the savages say there are two rivers, the one whereof we saw, having a fair entrance, but we had no time to discover it. Better harbors for shipping cannot be than here are. At the entrance of the bay are many rocks, and in all likelihood very good fishing-ground. Many, yea, most of the islands have been inhabited, some being cleared from end to end, but the people are all dead, or removed.

Our victual growing scarce, the wind coming fair, and having a light moon, we set out at evening and, through the goodness of God, came safely home before noon the day following.

A letter sent from New England to a friend in these parts, setting forth a brief and true declaration of the worth of that plantation; as also certain useful directions for such as intend a voyage into those parts.

Loving and Old Friend,[141]

Although I received no letter from you by this ship,[142] yet forasmuch as I know you expect the performance of my promise, which was, to write unto you truly and faithfully of all things, I have therefore at this time sent unto you accordingly, referring you for further satisfaction to our more large relations.[143]

You shall understand that in this little time that a few of us have been here, we have built seven dwelling-houses, and four for the use of the plantation, and have made preparation for divers others. We set the last spring some twenty acres of Indian corn, and sowed some six acres of barley and pease, and according to the manner of the Indians, we manured our ground with herrings, or rather shads, which we have in great abundance, and take with great ease at

---

[141] The following appears to be a covering letter which may have accompanied the manuscript journal when it was sent from Plymouth. Perhaps the "loving and old friend" of the author is George Morton, who presumably edited the relations for publication. See Introduction.

[142] The *Fortune*, first to follow the *Mayflower*.

[143] I. e., the preceding five narratives.

our doors. Our corn did prove well, and, God be praised, we had a good increase of Indian corn, and our barley indifferent good, but our pease not worth the gathering, for we feared they were too late sown. They came up very well, and blossomed, but the sun parched them in the blossom.

Our harvest being gotten in, our governor sent four men on fowling, that so we might after a special manner rejoice together after we had gathered the fruit of our labors.[144] They four in one day killed as much fowl as, with a little help beside, served the

---

[144] The following is the earliest description of the first Thanksgiving. The dates are not specified, nor is there specific mention of turkeys as comprising part of the feast, although they doubtless did.

company almost a week. At which time, amongst other recreations, we exercised our arms, many of the Indians coming amongst us, and among the rest their greatest king Massasoit, with some ninety men, whom for three days we entertained and feasted, and they went out and killed five deer, which they brought to the plantation and bestowed on our governor, and upon the captain and others. And although it be not always so plentiful as it was at this time with us, yet by the goodness of God, we are so far from want that we often wish you partakers of our plenty.

We have found the Indians very faithful in their covenant of peace with us, very loving and ready to pleasure us. We often go to them, and they come to us; some of us have been fifty miles by land in the country with them, the occasions and relations whereof you shall understand by our general and more full declaration of such things as are worth the noting. Yea, it hath pleased God so to possess the Indians with a fear of us, and love unto us, that not only the greatest king amongst them, called Massasoit, but also all the princes and peoples round about us, have either made suit unto us, or been glad of any occasion to make peace with us, so that seven of them at once have sent their messengers to us to that end.[145] Yea,

---

[145] The author here probably refers to the following document which was printed in 1669, in Morton's *New England's Memorial*: "September 13, Anno Dom. 1621. "Know all men by these presents, that we whose names are underwritten do acknowledge ourselves to be the loyal subjects of King James, King of Great Britain, France, and Ireland, Defender of the Faith, &c. In witness whereof, and as a testimonial of the same, we have subscribed our names or marks, as followeth: Ohquamehud, Cawnacome, Obbatinnua, Nattawahunt, Caunbatant, Chikkatabak, Quadequina, Huttamoiden, Apannow.

an Fle[146] at sea, which we never saw, hath also, together with the former, yielded willingly to be under the protection, and subjects to our sovereign lord King James. So that there is now great peace amongst the Indians themselves, which was not formerly, neither would have been but for us; and we for our parts walk as peaceably and safely in the wood as in the highways in England. We entertain them familiarly in our houses, and they as friendly bestowing their venison on us.

They are a people without any religion or knowledge of any God, yet very trusty, quick of apprehension, ripe-witted, just. The men and women go naked, only a skin about their middles.

For the temper of the air, here it agreeth well with that in England, and if there be any difference at all, this is somewhat hotter in summer. Some think it to be colder in winter, but I cannot out of experience so say; the air is very clear and not foggy, as hath been reported. I never in my life remember a more seasonable year than we have here enjoyed, and if we have once but kine[147], horses, and sheep, I make no question but men might live as contented here as in any part of the world. For fish and fowl, we have great abundance; fresh cod in the summer is but coarse meat with us; our bay is full of lobsters all the summer and affordeth variety of other fish; in September we can

---

[146] No such word occurs in either seventeenth-century English or local Indian languages. It is presumably a misprint for "Ile," i.e., *isle*, referring to Martha's Vineyard.
[147] *cattle*

take a hogshead of eels in a night, with small labor, and can dig them out of their beds all the winter. We have mussels and othus[148] at our doors. Oysters we have none near, but we can have them brought by the Indians when we will; all the spring-time the earth sendeth forth naturally very good sallet herbs.[149] Here are grapes, white and red, and very sweet and strong also. Strawberries, gooseberries, raspas,[150] etc. Plums of three sorts, with black and red, being almost as good as a damson; abundance of roses, white, red, and damask; single, but very sweet indeed. The country wanteth only industrious men to employ, for it would grieve your hearts if, as I, you had seen so many miles together by goodly rivers uninhabited, and withal, to consider those parts of the world wherein you live to be even greatly burdened with abundance of people.

These things I thought good to let you understand, being the truth of things as near as I could experimentally take knowledge of, and that you might on our behalf give God thanks who hath dealt so favorably with us.

Our supply of men[151] from you came the 9th of November 1621, putting in at Cape Cod, some eight or

---

[148] This also defies identification. Perhaps it is a misprint for *others*.

[149] I.e., salad greens.

[150] raspberries

[151] Thirty-five new settlers arrived on the *Fortune*, of whom some had set out with the original party but had to return to Plymouth, England, with the disabled ship *Speedwell*. The newly arrived heads of family were (in alphabetical order): John Adams, William Basset, William Beale, Edward Bompasse, Jonathan Brewster, Clement Briggs, John Cannon, William Conner, Thomas Cushman, Stephen Dean, Philip

ten leagues from us. The Indians that dwell thereabout were they who were owners of the corn which we found in caves, for which we have given them full content, and are in great league with them. They sent us word there was a ship near unto them, but thought it to be a Frenchman, and indeed for ourselves, we expected not a friend so soon. But when we perceived that she made for our bay, the governor commanded a great piece to be shot off, to call home such as were abroad at work; where-upon every man, yea, boy, that could handle a gun, were ready, with full resolution that if she were an enemy, we would stand in our just defense, not fearing them, but God provided better for us than we supposed. These came all in health, not any being sick by the way (otherwise than by sea-sickness) and so continue at this time, by the blessing of God; the good-wife Ford was delivered of a son the first night she landed, and both of them are very well.

When it pleaseth God, we are settled and fitted for the fishing business, and other trading; I doubt not but by the blessing of God the gain will give content to all. In the mean time, that we have gotten we have sent by this ship,[152] and though it be not much, yet it will

---

de la Noye, Thomas Flavell, Widow Ford, Robert Hicks, William Hilton, Bennet Morgan, Thomas Morton, Austin Nicholas, William Palmer, William Pitt, Thomas Prence, Moses Simonson, Hugh Stacie, James Stewart, William Tench, John Winslow, William Wright. Also aboard was Robert Cushman who presumably carried the manuscript journal back to England with him on the *Fortune's* return trip a month later.

[152] Bradford's *Of Plymouth Plantation* describes the *Fortune's* cargo as comprising beaver skins, clapboards, and sassafras, all of which was stolen by French privateers shortly before her arrival in London.

witness for us that we have not been idle, considering the smallness of our number all this summer. We hope the merchants will accept of it, and be encouraged to furnish us with things needful for further employment, which will also encourage us to put forth ourselves to the uttermost.

Now because I expect your coming unto us[153] with other of our friends, whose company we much desire, I thought good to advertise[154] you of a few things needful. Be careful to have a very good bread-room to put your biscuits in. Let your cask for beer and water be iron-bound for the first tire if not more; let not your meat be dry-salted—none can better do it than the sailors. Let your meal be so hard trod in your cask that you shall need an adz or hatchet to work it out with. Trust not too much on us for corn at this time, for by reason of this last company that came, depending wholly upon us, we shall have little enough till harvest; be careful to come by some of your meal to spend by the way—it will much refresh you. Build your cabins as open as you can, and bring good store of clothes and bedding with you. Bring every man a musket or fowling-piece; let your piece be long in the barrel, and fear not the weight of it, for most of our shooting is from stands. Bring juice of lemons, and take it fasting; it is of good use. For hot waters,

---

[153] George Morton, to whom this letter was presumably written, did come with the next party, on the ship *Anne*.

[154] advise

aniseed water is the best, but use it sparingly. If you bring any thing for comfort in the country, butter or sallet oil, or both is very good. Our Indian corn, even the coarsest, maketh as pleasant meat as rice, therefore spare that unless to spend by the way; bring paper and linseed oil for your windows, with cotton yarn for your lamps. Let your shot be most for big fowls, and bring store of powder and shot. I forbear further to write for the present, hoping to see you by the next return, so I take my leave, commending you to the Lord for a safe conduct unto us. Resting in him,

Your loving friend, E. W.[155]

Plymouth, in New England, this 11th of December, 1621.

---

[155] Presumably, Edward Winslow. See Introduction.

Chapter 6: A Settlement Manifesto

Editor Dwight B. Heath attributes this part of the Relation to Robert Cushman and states, "A long exposition of 'Reasons and considerations touching the lawfulness of removing out of England into the parts of America,' signed *R.C.*, is a thinly veiled promotional tract organized like a sermon, which cites Scripture to justify the plantation and to persuade others to follow."

It is interesting on its own, but it is also important for illustrating that these settlers of the Plymouth Colony were most certainly Godly people. Cushman's letter goes into great detail about the spiritual reasons for their emigration and settlement. He is also careful to clarify that the Pilgrims did not see themselves as new Israelites journeying to their own promised land (which they have been accused of). Cushman argues the need for land, industry, and the mission to spread the Gospel to the Americas.

Reasons and Considerations touching the lawfulness of removing out of England into the parts of America.

The Preamble

Forasmuch as many exceptions are daily made against the going into and inhabiting of foreign desert places, to the hindrances of plantations abroad, and the increase of distractions at home, it is not amiss that some which have been ear-witnesses of the exceptions made, and are either agents or abettors of such removals and plantations, do seek to give content to the world, in all things that possibly they can.

And although the most of the opposites are such as either dream of raising their fortunes here,[156] to that than which there is nothing more unlike, or such as affecting their home-born country so vehemently, as that they had rather with all their friends beg, yea, starve in it, than undergo a little difficulty in seeking abroad; yet are there some who, out of doubt in tenderness of conscience, and fear to offend God by running before they be called, are straitened and do straiten others from going to foreign plantations.

For whose cause especially, I have been drawn, out of my good affection to them, to publish some reasons that might give them content and satisfaction, and also stay and stop the willful and witty cavalier; and

---

[156] I.e., in England.

herein I trust I shall not be blamed of any godly wise, though through my slender judgment I should miss the mark, and not strike the nail on the head, considering it is the first attempt that hath been made (that I know of) to defend those enterprises. Reason would, therefore, that if any man of deeper reach and better judgment see further or otherwise, that he rather instruct me than deride me.

Cautions

And being studious for brevity, we must first consider that whereas God of old did call and summon our fathers by predictions, dreams, visions, and certain illuminations to go from their countries, places, and habitations, (Genesis 12:1, 2, & 35:1) to reside and dwell here or there, and to wander up and down from city to city, and land to land, according to his will and pleasure, now there is no such calling to be expected for any matter whatsoever, (Matthew 2:19) neither must any so much as imagine that there will now be any such thing. (Psalm 105:13) God did once so train up his people, but now he doth not (Hebrews 1:1, 2) but speaks in another manner, and so we must apply ourselves to God's present dealing, and not to his wonted dealing; and as the miracle of giving manna (Joshua 5:12) ceased when the fruits of the land became plenty, so God, having such a plentiful storehouse of directions in his holy word, there must not now any extraordinary revelations be expected. But now the ordinary examples and precepts of the Scriptures, reasonably and rightly understood and applied, must be the voice and word that must call us, press us, and direct us in every action.

Neither is there any land or possession now, like unto the possession which the Jews had in Canaan, (Genesis 17:8) being legally holy and appropriated unto a holy people, the seed of Abraham, in which they dwelt securely and had their days prolonged, it being by an immediate voice said, that he (the Lord) gave it them as a land of rest after their weary travels, and a type of eternal rest in heaven; but now there is no land of that sanctimony, no land so appropriated, none typical, much less any that can be said to be given of God to any nation as was Canaan, which they and their seed must dwell in, till God sendeth upon them sword or captivity.

But now we are all, in all places, strangers and pilgrims, travelers and sojourners, most properly, having no dwelling but in this earthen tabernacle; our dwelling is but a wandering, and our abiding but as a fleeting, and in a word our home is nowhere, but in the heavens, (II Corinthians 5:1, 2, 3) in that house not made with hands, whose maker and builder is God, and to which all ascend that love the coming of our Lord Jesus.

So were the Jews, but yet their temporal blessings and inheritances were more large than ours.

Though then there may be reasons to persuade a man to live in this or that land, yet there cannot be the same reasons which the Jews had, but now as natural, civil and religious bands tie men, so they must be bound, and as good reasons for things terrene[157] and heavenly appear, so they must be led.

Object.

And so here falleth in our question, how a man that is here born and bred, and hath lived some years, may remove himself into another country.

Answer 1. What persons may hence remove.

I answer, a man must not respect only to live, and do good to himself, but he should see where he can live to do most good to others; for, as one saith, "He whose living is but for himself, it is time he were dead." Some men there are who of necessity must here live, as being tied to duties, either to church, commonwealth, household, kindred, etc. But others, and that many, who do no good in none of those, nor can do none, as being not able, or not in favor, or as wanting opportunity, and live as outcasts, nobodies, eye-sores, eating but for themselves, teaching but themselves, and doing good to none, either in soul or body, and so

---

[157] *of or like earth; earthy*

147

pass over days, years, and months, yea, so live and so die. Now such should lift up their eyes and see whether there be not some other place and country to which they may go to do good and have use towards others of that knowledge, wisdom, humanity, reason, strength, skill, faculty, etc., which God hath given them for the service of others and his own glory.

2. Why they should remove.

Reason 1

But not to pass the bounds of modesty so far as to name any, though I confess I know many, who sit here still (Luke 19:20) with their talent in a napkin, having notable endowments both of body and mind, and might do great good if they were in some places, which here do none, nor can do none, and yet through fleshly fear, niceness,[158] straightness of heart, etc., sit still and look on and will not hazard a dram of health, nor a day of pleasure, nor an hour of rest to further the knowledge and salvation of the sons of Adam in that New World, where a drop of the knowledge of Christ is most precious, which is here not set by. Now what shall we say to such a profession of Christ, to which is joined no more denial of a man's self?

---

[158] shyness

Object.

But some will say, what right have I to go live in the heathens' country?

Answer

Letting pass the ancient discoveries, contracts and agreements which our Englishmen have long since made in those parts, together with the acknowledgment of the histories and chronicles of other nations, who profess the land of America from the Cape de Florida unto the Bay of Canada (which is south and north three hundred leagues and upwards, and east and west further than yet hath been discovered) is proper to the King of England—yet letting that pass, lest I be thought to meddle further than it concerns me, or further than I have discerning, I will mention such things as are within my reach, knowledge, sight and practice, since I have travailed in these affairs.

Reason 2.

And first, seeing we daily pray for the conversion of the heathens, we must consider whether there be not some ordinary means and course for us to take to convert them, or whether prayer for them be only referred to God's extraordinary work from heaven. Now it seemeth unto me that we ought also to endeavor and use the means to convert them, and the means cannot be used unless we go to them or they come to us; to us they cannot come, our land is full; to them we may go, their land is empty.

Reason 3.

This then is a sufficient reason to prove our going thither to live lawful: their land is spacious and void, and there are few and do but run over the grass, as do also the foxes and wild beasts. They are not industrious, neither have art, science, skill or faculty to use either the land or the commodities of it, but all spoils, rots, and is marred for want of manuring, gathering, ordering, etc. As the ancient patriarchs therefore removed from straighter places into more roomy, where the land lay idle and waste, and none used it, though there dwelt inhabitants by them, (as Genesis 13:6,11,12, and 34:21, and 41:20), so is it lawful now to take a land which none useth, and make use of it.

Reason 4. This is to be considered as respecting New England, and the territories about the plantation.

And as it is a common land or unused, and undressed country, so we have it by common consent, composition and agreement, which agreement is double. First, the imperial governor Massasoit, whose circuits in likelihood are larger than England and Scotland, hath acknowledged the King's Majesty of England to be his master and commander, and that once in my hearing, yea, and in writing, under his hand to Captain

Standish, both he and many other kings which are under him, as Paomet, Nauset, Cummaquid, Narraganset, Nemasket, etc., with divers others that dwell about the bays of Patuxet and Massachusetts. Neither hath this been accomplished by threats and blows, or shaking of sword and sound of trumpet, for as our faculty that way is small, and our strength less, so our warring with them is after another manner, namely by friendly usage, love, peace, honest and just carriages, good counsel, etc., that so we and they may not only live in peace in that land, (Psalm 110:3, & 48:3) and they yield subjection to an earthly prince, but that as voluntaries they may be persuaded at length to embrace the Prince of Peace, Christ Jesus, and rest in peace with him forever.

Secondly, this composition is also more particular and applicatory, as touching ourselves there inhabiting: the emperor, by a joint consent, hath promised and appointed us to live at peace where we will in all his dominions, taking what place we will, and as much land as we will, and bringing as many people as we will, and that for these two causes. First, because we are the servants of James, King of England, whose the land (as he confesseth) is; second, because he hath found us just, honest, kind and peaceable, and so loves our company; yea, and that in these things there is no dissimulation on his part, nor fear of breach (except our security engender in them some unthought of treachery, or our uncivility provoke them to anger) is most plain in other relations,[159] which show that the things they did were more out of love than out of fear.

It being then, first, a vast and empty chaos; secondly, acknowledged the right of our sovereign king; thirdly, by a peaceable composition in part possessed of divers of his loving subjects, I see not who can doubt or call in question the lawfulness of inhabiting or dwelling there, but that it may be as lawful for such as are not tied upon some special occasion here, to live there as well as here. Yea, and as the enterprise is weighty and difficult, so the honor is more worthy, to plant a rude wilderness, to enlarge the honor and fame of our dread sovereign, but chiefly to display the efficacy and power of the Gospel, both in zealous preaching, professing, and wise walking under it, before the faces of these poor blind infidels.

As for such as object the tediousness of the voyage thither, the danger of pirates' robbery, of the savages' treachery, etc., these are but lions in the way, (Proverbs 22:13) and it were well for such men if they were in heaven, for who can show them a place in this world where iniquity shall not (Psalm 49:5) compass them at the heels, and where they shall have a day without grief, or a lease of life for a moment; (Matthew 6:34) and who can tell, but God, what dangers may lie at our doors, even in our native country, or what plots may be abroad, or when God

---

[159] That is, the preceding journal.

will cause our sun to go down at noon-days, and in the midst of our peace and security, lay upon us (Amos 8:9) some lasting scourge for our so long neglect and contempt of his most glorious Gospel?

Object

But we have here great peace, plenty of the Gospel, and many sweet delights, and variety of comforts.

Answer

True indeed, and far be it from us to deny and diminish the least of these mercies, but have we rendered unto God thankful obedience for this long peace, whilst other peoples have been at wars? (II Chronicles 32:25) Have we not rather murmured, repined, and fallen at wars amongst ourselves, whilst our peace hath lasted with foreign power? Was there ever more suits in law, more envy, contempt and reproach than nowadays? Abraham and Lot departed asunder (Genesis 13:9, 10) when there fell a breach betwixt them, which was occasioned by the straightness[160] of the land; and surely, I am persuaded that howsoever the frailties of men are principal in all contentions, yet the straightness of the place is such as each man is fain to pluck his means, as it were, out of his neighbor's throat; there is such pressing and oppressing in town and country, about farms, trades,

---

[160] *Being crowded*

traffic, etc., so as a man can hardly any where set up a trade but he shall pull down two of his neighbors.

The towns abound with young tradesmen, and the hospitals are full of the ancient; the country is replenished with new farmers, and the almshouses are filled with old laborers; many there are who get their living with bearing burdens, but more are fain to burden the land with their whole bodies. Multitudes get their means of life by prating[161], and so do numbers more by begging. Neither come these straits upon men always through intemperance, ill husbandry, indiscretion, etc., as some think, but even the most wise, sober, and discreet men go often to the wall, when they have done their best, wherein, as God's providence swayeth all, so it is easy to see that the straightness of the place, having in it so many strait hearts, cannot but produce such effects more and more, so as every indifferent minded man should be ready to say with father Abraham, "Take thou the right hand, and I will take the left."

Let us not thus oppress, straiten, and afflict one another, but seeing there is a spacious land, the way to which is through the sea, we will end this difference in a day.

That I speak nothing about the bitter contention that hath been about religion, by writing, disputing, and inveighing earnestly one against another, the heat of

---

161 *Talking idly*

which zeal, if it were turned against the rude barbarism of the heathens, it might do more good in a day than it hath done here in many years. Neither of the little love to the Gospel, and profit which is made by the preachers in most places, which might easily drive the zealous to the heathens who, no doubt, if they had but a drop of that knowledge which here flieth about the streets, would be filled with exceeding great joy and gladness, as that they would even pluck the kingdom of heaven by violence, and take it as it were, by force.

The last let.[162]

The greatest let that is yet behind is the sweet fellowship of friends, and the satiety of bodily delights.

But can there be two nearer friends almost than Abraham and Lot, or than Paul and Barnabas? And yet, upon as little occasions as we have here, they departed asunder, two of them being patriarchs of the church of old; the other the apostles of the church which is new, and their covenants were such as it seemeth might bind as much as any covenant between men at this day, and yet to avoid greater inconveniences they departed asunder.

Neither must men take so much thought for the flesh, as not to be pleased except they can pamper their bodies with variety of dainties. Nature is content with little, and health is much endangered by mixtures

---

[162] hindrance

upon the stomach. The delights of the palate do often inflame the vital parts as the tongue setteth afire the whole body. (James 3:6)

Secondly, varieties here are not common to all, but many good men are glad to snap at a crust. The rent-taker lives on sweet morsels, but the rent-payer eats a dry crust often with watery eyes, and it is nothing to say what some one of a hundred hath, but what the bulk, body and commonalty hath, which I warrant you is short enough.

And they also which now live so sweetly, hardly will their children attain to that privilege, but some circumventor or other will outstrip them, and make them sit in the dust, to which men are brought in one age, but cannot get out of it again in seven generations.

To conclude, without all partiality, the present consumption which groweth upon us here, whilst the land groaneth under so many close-fisted and unmerciful men, being compared with the easiness, plainness and plentifulness in living in those remote places, may quickly persuade any man to a liking of this course, and to practice a removal, which being done by honest, godly and industrious men, they shall there be right heartily welcome, but for other of dissolute and profane life, their rooms are better than their companies. For if here[163], where the Gospel hath

---

[163] *England*

been so long and plentifully taught, they are yet
frequent in such vices as the heathen would shame to
speak of, what will they be when there is less restraint
in word and deed? My only suit to all men is, that
whether they live there or here, they would learn to
use this world as they used it not, keeping faith and a
good conscience, both with God and men, that when
the day of account shall come, they may come forth as
good and fruitful servants, and freely be received, and
enter into the joy of their Master.

R. C.[164]

FINIS

---

[164] Presumably, Robert Cushman. See Introduction.

Chapter 7: Plymouth and beyond

This *Relation* is but one year's history of the Plymouth Colony in Massachusetts. Despite rough beginnings, and more than half of the original settlers dying, the settlement went on to prosper and grow.

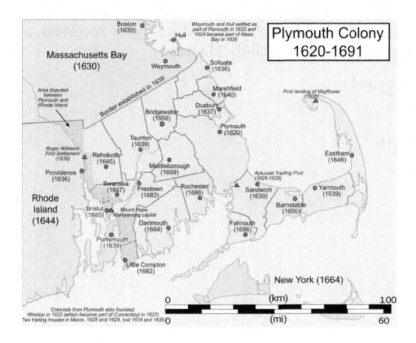

In 1630, more Puritans settled in Boston with John Winthrop. In time, their population spread into what would become Connecticut, New Hampshire, Rhode Island and Maine, and eventually beyond the limits of New England.

While many other settlements were growing up in the Colonies, the Puritan settlements were different for a few reasons:

1. They were overwhelming families, and not just men
2. There were more commoners and less English nobility
3. They were dedicated to a life of holiness
4. They strove to maintain peace with the surrounding Indian tribe whenever possible

While the Puritans have been remembered as stuffy and somber, their true reputation should be that of striving for holiness. They were also industrious, literate, and visionary. And though their specific brand of Christian citizenship is not as widespread today, History.com accurately states, "[Puritanism] survived, perhaps most conspicuously, in the secular form of self-reliance, moral rigor and political localism that became, by the Age of Enlightenment, virtually the definition of Americanism.

What also survived are the foundations of the United States of America: freedom of religion, freedom of speech, capitalism, and a Republican form of government.

Alexi de Tocqueville, who visited America in the early 19th century, wrote, "The foundation of New England was something new in the world" because Puritanism was almost as much a political theory as a religious doctrine."

We can trace the literal foundation of the United States back to the Plymouth colony, and that colony's roots go back the world-changing invention we know as the printing press.

ENDNOTE

ⁱ A SERMON
Preached at PLYMOUTH, *in* New England, 1621.

1 CORINTHIANS, 10. 24: LET NO MAN SEEK HIS OWN: BUT EVERY MAN ANOTHER'S WEALTH.

The occasion of these words of the Apostle *Paul*, was because of the abuses which were in the Church of *Corinth*. Which abuses arose chiefly through swelling pride, self-love and conceitedness, for although this church was planted by *Paul* and watered by *Apollos*, and much increased by the Lord; yet the sower of tares was not wanting to stir up evil workers and fleshly minded hypocrites, under a shew of godliness, and with angel-like holiness in appearance, to creep in amongst them to disturb their peace, try their soundness, and prove their constancy. And this the Apostle complains of very often: as first, in their carnal divisions, chap. 1. then in their extolling their eloquent teachers, and despising *Paul*, chap. 4. Then in their offensive going to Law, before the heathen judges, chap. 6. Then in eating things offered to idols, to the destroying of the tender consciences of their brethren, chap. 8. Then in their insatiable love feasts, in the time and place of their church meetings, the rich which could together feed to fulness, despising and contemning the poor, that had not to lay it on as they had, chap. 11. Finally in both the epistles, he very often nippeth them for their pride, and self-love, straightness and censoriousness, so that in the last chapter he willeth them again and again to prove, try and examine themselves, to see whether Christ were in them or not, for howsoever many of them seemed, as thousands do at this day to soar aloft, and go with full sail to Heaven: yet as men that row in boats, set their faces one way, when yet their whole body goeth apace another way: so there are many which set such a face upon religion, and have their mouth full of great swelling words: as if they would even blow open the doors of heaven, despising all humble minded and broken-hearted people, as weak, simple, sottish, &c. when yet notwithstanding, these blusterers, which seem to go so fast, and leave all others behind them, if like these glosing *Corinthians*, they carry affectedly their own glory with them, and seem thus to stand for the glory of God. What do they else but join flesh to spirit, serving not God for naught, but for wages, and so serving their bellies, whose end will be damnation, except a speedy and sound remedy be thought of, which remedy is even that which our Saviour teacheth the rich young gallant, and which *Paul* here prescribeth, in willing them not to seek their own, but every man another's wealth, which physic is as terrible to carnal professors, as abstinence from drink is to a man that hath the dropsy; and it is a sure note, that a man is sick of this disease of self-love, if this be grievous to him, as appeareth in the man whom Christ bid sell that he had, and he went away very sorrowful, yet surely this vein must be pricked, and this humor let out, else it will spoil all, it will infect both soul and body, yea, and the contagion of it is such (as we shall see anon) as will even hazard the welfare of that society where self seekers and self lovers are.

As God then did direct this Apostle to lay down this brief direction as a remedy for that evil in *Corinth*, so you may think it is by God's special providence, that I am now to speak unto you from this text: and say in your hearts, surely something is amiss this way: let us know it and amend it.

The parts of this text are two. 1. A *Dehortation*. 2. An *Exhortation*. The Dehortation, *Let no man seek his own*. The Exhortation, *But every man another's wealth*.

In handling of which, I will first, open the words. Secondly, gather the doctrine. Thirdly illustrate the doctrine by scriptures, experience and reasons. Fourthly apply the same, to every one his portion.

The proper drift of the Apostle here is not to tax the *Corinthians*, for seeking their own evil ends in evil actions, but for aiming at themselves, and their own benefits in actions lawful, and that appeareth in the former verse, where he saith, *All things are lawful, &c.* viz. all such things as now we speak of, to eat any of God's creatures, offered to idols or not, to feast and be merry together, to shew love and kindness to this or that person, &c. but when by such means we seek ourselves, and have not a charitable loving and reverent regard of others, then they are unexpedient, unprofitable, yea unlawful, and must be forborne, and he that hath not learned to deny himself even the very use of lawful things, when it tendeth to the contempt, reproach, grief,

163

offence and shame of his other brethren and associates, hath learned nothing aright, but is, apparently, a man that seeks himself, and against whom the Apostle here dealeth most properly.

The manner of the speech, may seem as counsel left at liberty: as Mat. 27. 49. And in our ordinary speech, we think they be but weak charges, which are thus delivered, let a man do this, or let him do that. But we must learn the apostle's modesty, and know that whatsoever the terms seem to imply, yet even this and other the like in this epistle, are most absolute charges: as, *Let a man esteem of us, as the ministers of Christ, chap. 41.* That is, a man ought so to esteem of us. *Let a man examine himself, 1 Cor. 11. 28.* That is, as if he said, a man must examine himself. *Let your women keep silence in the churches, 1 Cor. 14, 34.* that is, they ought so to do.

The meaning then summarily is, as if he said, the bane of all these mischiefs which arise among you is, that men are too cleaving to themselves and their own matters, and disregard and contemn all others: and therefore I charge you, let this self seeking be left off, and turn the stream another way, namely, seek the good of your brethren, please them, honor them, reverence them, for otherwise it will never go well amongst you.

Obj. But doth not the Apostle elsewhere say? *That he, which careth not for his own, is worse than an infidel. 1 Tim. 5. 8.*

Ans. True, but by (own) there, he meaneth properly, a man's kindred, and here by (own) he meaneth properly a man's self.

Secondly, he there especially taxeth such as were negligent in their labors and callings, and so made themselves unable to give relief and entertainment to such poor widows and orphans as were of their own flesh and blood.

Thirdly, be it so, that some man should even neglect his own self, his own wife, children, friends, &c. And give that he had to strangers, that were but some rare vice, in some one unnatural man, and if this vice slay a thousand, self-love slayeth ten thousands.

And this the wisdom of God did well foresee, and hath set no caveats in the scriptures either to tax men, or forewarn them from loving others, neither saith God any where, let no man seek out the good of another, but let no man seek his own, and every where in the scriptures he hath set watch words against self good, self-profit, self-seeking, &c. And thus the sense being cleared, I come to the doctrine.

Doct. 1. *All men are too apt and ready to seek themselves too much, and to prefer their own matters and causes beyond the due and lawful measure, even to excess and offence against God, yea danger of their own souls.*

And this is true not only in wicked men which are given over of God to vile lusts, as *Absalom* in getting favor in his father's court: *Jereboam*, in settling his kingdom fast in *Samaria*, *Ahab* in vehement seeking *Naboth's* vineyard, but men, otherwise godly, have through frailty been foiled herein, and many thousands which have a shew of godliness, are lovers of themselves: *David* was about to seek himself when he was going to kill *Naball*: *Asa* in putting *Hanani* in prison: *Josiah* when he would go to war with *Necho*, against the counsel of God, and reason; *Peter* when he dissembled about the ceremonies of the law, yea and *Paul* complains of all his followers (*Timothy* excepted) that they sought their own too inordinately.

And why else are these caveats in the scriptures, but to warn the godly that they be not tainted herewith? as, *Look not every man on his own things, but on the things of another: Love seeketh not her own things. Be not desirous of vain glory, &c.* Philip. 2. 4. 1 Cor. 13. 6. Gal. 5. 26.

Yea and doth not experience teach, that even amongst professors of religion, almost all the love and favor that is shewed unto others is with a secret aim at themselves, they will take pains to do a man good, provided that he will take twice so much for them, they will give a penny so as it may advantage them a pound, labor hard so as all the profit may come to themselves, else they are heartless and feeble. The vain and corrupt heart of man cannot better be resembled then by a belly-god, host, or innkeeper which welcometh his guests with smilings, and salutations, and a thousand welcomes, and rejoiceth greatly to have their company to dice, cards, eat, drink, and be merry, but should not the box be paid, the pot be filling, and the money telling, all this while, the epicure's joy would soon be turned into sorrow, and his smiles turned into frowns, and the door set open, and their absence craved: even so men blow the bellows hard, when they have an iron of their own a heating, work hard whilst their own house is in building, dig hard whilst their own garden is in planting, but is it so as the profit must go

166

wholly or partly to others; their hands wax feeble, their hearts wax faint, they grow churlish, and give cross answers, like *Naball*, they are sour, discontent, and nothing will please them. And where is that man to be found, that will disperse abroad, and cast his bread upon the waters, that will lend, looking for nothing again, that will do all duties to other freely and cheerfully in conscience to God, and love unto men, without his close and secret ends or aiming at himself; such a man, out of doubt, is a black swan, a white crow almost, and yet such shall stand before God with boldness at the last day, when others which have sought themselves, though for love of themselves they have sought heaven, yea, and through self-love persuaded themselves they should find it, yet wanting love unto others, they will be found as sounding brass, and as a tinkling cimbal, and whilst they have neglected others, and not cared how others live, so as themselves may fare well, they will be found amongst them, that the Lord will say unto, *I know you not, depart ye cursed into everlasting fire*, Mat. 25. 41. 42.

But that I may not walk in generalities, the particular ways by which men seek their own are these: First, such as are covetous, seek their own by seeking riches, wealth, money, as *Felix* pretending love unto *Paul*, sent for him often, but it was in hope of money. Many there are who say, *who will shew us any good*, Psal. 4. 7. And pretend religion, as some of the Jews did the keeping of the Sabbath, which yet cried out, when will the Sabbath be done, that we may sell corn, and get gain; if a man can tell how to get gold out of a flint, and silver out of the adamant, no pains shall be spared, no time shall be neglected, for gold is their hope, and the wedge of gold is their confidence, their hearts are set upon the pelf of this world, and for love of it, all things are let slip, even all duties to God or men, they care not how basely they serve, how wretchedly they neglect all others, so as they may get wealth: pinch who will, and wring who will; all times are alike with them, and they run for the bribe and *Gehazie*; and this is the first way that men seek their own.

Now the contrary is seen in *Nehemiah*, who when the people were hard put to it, and the land raw, he took not the duties which were due to him being a magistrate, he bought no land, nor grew rich, for it was no time: but he maintained at his table many of his brethren the Jews, and so spent even his own proper goods. And *Paul* sought no man's gold nor silver, but though he had authority, yet he took not bread of the churches, but labored with his hands: and why? It was no time to take, some churches were poor and stood in want, as *Thessalonica*, others were in danger to be preyed upon by covetous belly-gods, as *Corinth*: and therefore he saw it no fit time now to take any thing of them.

And indeed here is the difference between a covetous worldling, and an honest thrifty Christian, it is lawful sometimes for men to gather wealth, and grow rich, even as there was a time for *Joseph* to store up corn, but a godly and sincere Christian will see when this time is, and will not hoard up when he seeth others of his brethren and associates to want, but then is a time, if he have any thing to fetch it out and disperse it, but the covetous gathers goods, he like *Achan* covets all that he seeth; and neglects no time, but gathers still and holds all fast, and if it were to save the life of his brother, his bags must not be diminished, nor his chests lighted, nor his field set to sale, gather as much as he can, but it's death to diminish the least part of it.

2. The second way by which men seek their own, is when they seek ease, or pleasure, as the *Scribes* and *Pharisees*, who would not touch the burden with one of their fingers; for there is a generation, which think to have more in this world then *Adam's* felicity in innocency, being born (as they think) to take their pleasures, and their ease, let the roof of the house drop through, they stir not; let the field be overgrown with weeds, they care not, they must not foul their hand, nor wet their foot, it's enough for them to say, Go you, not let us go, though never so much need; such idle drones, are intolerable in a settled commonwealth, much more in a commonwealth which is but as it were in the bud; of what earth I pray thee art thou made, of any better than the other of the sons of *Adam*? And canst thou see other of thy brethren toil their hearts out, and thou sit idle at home, or takest thy pleasure abroad? Remember the example of *Uriah*, who would not take his ease nor his pleasure, though the King required him, and why? Because his brethren, his associates, better men than himself (as he esteemed them) were under hard labors and conditions, lay in the field in tents, caves, &c.

3. The third way is when men seek their own bellies, as some did in the Apostles' times, which went about with new doctrines and devices, knowing that the people had itching ears, and would easily entertain and willingly feed such novelists, which brought in dissensions, schisms, and contentions, and such were rocks, or pillars in their love-feasts, as *Jude* speaketh, *ver. 12.* They were shadows in God's service, but when feasting came, then they were substances, then they were in their element. And certainly there are some men which shape even their religion, human

state, and all, even as the belly cheer is best, and that they must have, else all heart and life is gone; let all conscience, care of others go, let *Lazarus* starve at the gate, let *Joseph's* affliction be increased, they must have their dishes, their dainties, or no content. The contrary was seen in *Nehemiah,* who would not take his large portion allotted to the governor, because he knew it went short with others of his brethren; and *Uriah* would not receive the King's present, and go banquet with his wife, because he knew the whole host his brethren were fain to snap short in the fields.

And the difference between a temperate good man, and a belly-god is this: A good man will not eat his morsels alone, especially, if he have better than others, but if by God's providence, he have gotten some meat which is better than ordinary, and better than his other brethren, he can have no rest in himself, except he make others partake with him. But a belly-god will slop all in his own throat, yea, though his neighbor come in and behold him eat, yet his griple-gut shameth not to swallow all. And this may be done sometimes, as well in mean fare as in greater dainties, for all countries afford not alike.

4. The fourth way by which men seek their own, is by seeking outward honor, fame and respect with men; as King *Saul* when he had lost all respect and favor with God, then thought to give content to his heart by being honored before the Elders of the people; and it is wonderful to see how some men are *desirous of vain glory, Gal.* 5. 26. And how earnestly they seek praise, favor, and respect with men, and can have no quiet longer than their worldly favor lasteth, and that they will have what dishonor soever come to God, or disgrace unto men, yea, they will disgrace, reproach, and

disdain others, to gain honor and advancement to themselves, yea, they will make bold with the Scriptures and Word of God, to wrest and wring, and slight it over for their credit's sake. And let a man mark some men's talk, stories, discourses, &c. and he shall see their whole drift is to extol and set out themselves, and get praise and commendation of men.

Now the contrary was seen in *Paul*, he saith, *He needed no letters of commendations*, 2 Cor. 3. 2. And again, *He is not affected with men's praise*, 1 Cor. 10. 12. And here is indeed the difference between an humble-minded Christian, and a proud self-lover; an humble man often hath praise, as *David*, *Hezekiah*, and *Josiah*, but he seeks it not, he desires it not, he is content to go without it, he loves not the praise of men, for he knows it but froth and vanity: but a proud self-lover, he seeks it still, get it or not get it, and if he get it he is fully satisfied, if he get it not he hangs his head like a bull-rush, and hath no comfort.

5. The fifth way by which men seek their own, is *by seeking to have their wills*; as the wrong doers in *Corinth*, who thought it not enough to do wrong and harm to their brethren, but to have their wills enough of them, drew them before the Heathen magistrates.

And truly some men are so prince-like, or rather Papal, that their very will and word is become a law, and if they have said it, it must be so, else there is no rest or quietness to be had, let never so many reasons be brought to the contrary, it is but fighting with the wind. They are like the obstinate Jews, who when against God's law, and reason, they asked a King, though *Samuel* shewed them that it would turn in the end to their own smart, yet still held the conclusion, and said, nay, *But we will have a King*, 1 Sam. 8. 19. Thus men are caught by their own words, and insnared by the straightness of their own hearts, and it is death to them not to have their wills, and howsoever sometimes (like *Jezebel*) they are cut short of their purposes, yet self-willed men will strut and swell like *Absalom*, saying neither *good nor bad*, 2 Sam. 13. 22. but hope for the day, and threaten like prophane *Esau*, Gen. 27. 41. Now the contrary is seen in *David*, though a prince, a captain, a warrior, who having said, yea sworn, that he would kill *Nabal*, and all his family that day, yet upon reasonable counsel given, and that by a weak woman, he changed his mind, altered his purpose, and returned, without striking one stroke, an example rare, and worthy imitation; and when men are sick of will, let them think of *David*, it was his grace and honor to go back from his word and practice, when reason came. So was it *Herod's* disgrace and shame to hold his word and will against reason and conscience, *Math. 14. 8, 9.*

Quest. But some men happily will say unto me, It is true, that men seek their own by all these ways, *But what should be the reason and cause of this? that men seek so earnestly themselves, in seeking riches, honor, ease, belly-cheer, will, &c. something there is that carrieth them.*

Ans. True, and the reasons and causes are specially these three:

First, pride and high conceitedness, when men overvalue themselves: and this made *Absalom* to seek his father's kingdom, because he thought himself worthy of it. *2 Sam. 15. 4.* This made *Haman* so sore vexed, because *Mordecai* bowed not to him, because he highly valued himself, *Esther, 3. 5.*

And surely that which a man valueth much, he giveth much respect to, and so it is a sure sign that a man loves himself most when he giveth most to himself; and some intolerable proud persons even think all the world is for them, and all their purposes and endeavors shew what a large conceit they have of themselves.

Secondly, want of due consideration and valuation of other men's endowments, abilities and deserts; when men pass those things by, though they have both seen, heard, and felt them; as *Pharaoh's* butler forgot *Joseph's* eminency when he was restored to his place, *Gen. 40. 23.* So men used to write their own good actions in brass, but other men's in ashes, never remembering nor considering the pains, labor, good properties, &c. which others have, and so they have no love to them, but only to themselves; as if God had made all other men unreasonable beasts, and them only reasonable men.

Thirdly, want of heavenly conversation, and spiritual eye to behold the glory, greatness, and majesty, and goodness of God; as the Queen of *Sheba*, thought highly of her own glory, wisdom and happiness, till she saw *Solomon's* wisdom and glory, and then she cried out, not of the happiness of her own servants, but of his servants that stood before him, *1 Kings 10. 7, 8.* And verily, if men were conversant courtiers in Heaven, they would cry out with *Paul*, Rom. 11. 33. *Oh the depth of the riches, wisdom, and knowledge of God, &c.* and would be ashamed of their own sinfulness, nakedness and misery; for, as countrymen which never saw the state of cities, nor the glory of courts, admire even their own country Orders: And as the savages here which are clad in skins, and creep in woods and holes, think their own brutish and inhuman life the best, which if they saw and did rightly apprehend the benefit of comely humanity, the sweetness of religion and the service of God, they would even shamefully hide themselves from the eye of all noble Christians. Even so, if men in serious contemplation, by the eye of faith, would behold the glory of God, and what great riches, beauty, fulness, perfection, power, dignity and greatness is in God, they would leave admiring of themselves, and seeking of themselves, and would say with *David, What am I? And what is my father's house? that thou shouldest thus bless me?* 2 Sam. 7. 18. Yea *What is man? or the son of man that thou so regardest him?* Psal. 8. 3.

But it is time to come to apply these things more particularly to ourselves, and see what Use is to be made of them:

Use 1. Is it so, that God seeth a proneness in all the sons of *Adam*, to seek themselves too much, and hath given them warnings and watch-words thereof, as we have heard, and doth experience confirm it? Then hence are reproved a number of men, who think they can never shew love enough to themselves, nor seek their own enough, but think all cost, charges, cherishing, praise, honor, &c. too little for them, and no man needeth to say to them, as *Peter* did to Christ, *favor thy self*; but if they do a little for another man, they account it a great matter, though it be but a morsel of bread, or a single penny; but no varieties of dainties is too good for them, no silk, purple, cloth, or stuff is too good to clothe them, the poor man's idleness and ill husbandry is oft thrown in his dish, but their own carnal delights and fleshy wantonness is never thought upon: and why? Because they think even God and man owes all to them, but they owe nothing to none. Why, thou foolish and besotted man, hath not the Holy Ghost read it in the very face of every son of *Adam*, that he is too apt to seek his own, and art thou wiser than God, to think thou never seekest thine own enough? or dreamest thou that thou art made of other, and better mettle than other men are? Surely, I know no way to escape, having of corruption to thy father, and the worm to thy sister and brother. And if God had any where in all the Scriptures said, love thyself, make much of thyself, provide for one, &c. there were some reason for thee to take up the niggard's proverbs, *Every man for himself, and God for us all; Charity beginneth at home, &c.* But God never taught thee these things; No, they are Satan's positions. Doth God ever commend a man for carnal love of himself? Nay he brands it, and disgraceth it, as *self love, taking thought for the flesh; loving of pleasure, &c.* Rom. 13. 14, 2 Tim. 34.

Obj. It is a point of good natural policy, for a man to care and provide for himself.

Ans. Then the most fools have most natural policy, for you see not the greatest drones and novices, either in church, or commonwealth, to be the greatest scratchers and scrapers, and gatherers of riches? Are they not also for the most part, best fed and clad? And live they not most easily? What shall I say? Even hogs, dogs, and brute beasts know their own ease, and can seek that which is good for themselves; and what doth this shifting, progging, and fat feeding which some use, more resemble any thing than the fashion of hogs? And so let it be what natural policy it will.

Use 2. If God see this disease of self-love so dangerous in us, then it standeth us all in hand to suspect ourselves, and so to seek out the root of this disease, that it may be cured. If a learned physician, shall see by our countenance and eye, that we have some dangerous disease growing on us, our hearts will smite us, and we will bethink ourselves where the most grief lieth, and how it should come, whether with cold, heat, surfeit, over-flowing of blood, or through grief, melancholy, or any such way, and every man will bestir himself to get rid of it, and will prevent always that which feeds the disease, and cherish all courses that would destroy it.

Now, how much more ought we to bestir ourselves, for this matter of self love, since God himself hath cast all our waters, and felt all our pulses, and pronounceth us all dangerously sick of this disease? Believe it, God cannot lie, nor be deceived; He that made the heart, doth not he know it? Let every man's heart smite him, and let him fall to the examination of himself and see first, whether he love not riches and worldly wealth too much, whether his heart be not too jocund at the coming of it in, and too heavy at the going of it out, for if you find it so there is great danger, if thou canst not buy as if thou possessed not, and use this world as though thou used it not, (*1 Cor. 7. 30, 31.*) thou art sick, and had need to look to it. So, if thou lovest thine ease and pleasure, see whether thou can be content to receive at God's hands evil as well as good, (*Job 2. 10.*) whether thou have learned as well to abound as to want, (*Phil. 4. 10.*) as well to endure hard labor, as to live at ease; and art as willing to go to the house of mourning as to the house of mirth, (*Eccl. 7. 6.*) for, else, out of doubt, thou lovest thy carnal pleasure and ease too much.

Again, see whether thy heart cannot be as merry, and thy mind as joyful, and thy countenance as cheerful, with coarse fare, with pulse, with bread and water (if God offer thee no better, nor the times afford other) as if thou had the greatest dainties: (*Dan. 1. 15.*) So also whether thou can be content as well with scorns of men, when thou hast done well, as with their praises, so if thou can with comfort and good conscience say, I pass little for man's judgment; whether thou can do thy duty that God requireth, and despise the shame, referring thyself unto God, for if thou be disheartened, discouraged, and weakened in any duty because of men's dispraises, its a sign thou lovest thyself too much.

So for the will, if thou can be content to give way even from that which thou hast said shall be, yea, vowed shall be, when better reason cometh, and hast that reverence of other men, as that when it standeth but upon a matter of will, thou art as willing their wills should stand as thine, and art not sad, churlish, or discontented, (*1 Kings 21. 4.*) but cheerful in thine heart, though thy will be crossed, it is a good sign, but if not, thou art sick of a self-will, and must purge it out. I the rather press these things, because I see many men both wise and religious, which yet are so tainted with this pestilent self-love, as that it is in them even as a dead fly to the apothecaries' ointment, spoiling the efficacy of all their graces, making their lives uncomfortable to themselves, and unprofitable to others, being neither fit for church nor commonwealth, but have even their very souls in hazard thereby, and therefore who can say too much against it.

It is reported, that there are many men gone to that other plantation in *Virginia*, which, whilst they lived in *England*, seemed very religious, zealous, and conscionable; and have now lost even the sap of grace, and edge to all goodness; and are become mere worldlings. This testimony I believe to be partly true, and amongst many causes of it, this self-love is not the least. It is indeed a matter of some commendation for a man to remove himself out of a thronged place into a wide wilderness; to take in hand so long and dangerous a journey, to be an instrument to carry the Gospel and humanity among the brutish heathen; but there may be many goodly shews and glosses and yet a pad in the straw, men may make a great appearance of respect unto God, and yet but dissemble with him, having their own lusts carrying them: and, out of doubt, men that have taken in hand hither to come, out of discontentment in regard of their estates in *England*; and aiming at great matters here, affecting it to be gentlemen, landed men, or hoping for office, place, dignity, or fleshly liberty; let the shew be what it will, the substance is naught, and that bird of self-love which was hatched at home, if it be not looked to, will eat out the life of all grace and goodness: and though men have escaped the danger of the sea, and that cruel mortality, which swept away so many of our loving friends and brethren; yet except they purge out this self-love, a worse mischief is prepared for them: And who knoweth whether God in mercy have delivered those just men which here departed, from the evils to come; and from unreasonable men, in whom there neither was, nor is, any comfort, but grief, sorrow, affliction, and misery, till they cast out this spawn of self-love.

But I have dwelt too long upon this first part; I come now to the second, which concerns an Exhortation, as I shewed you, in the Division.

But every man another's wealth.

In direct opposition, he should say, *Let every man seek another's,* but the first part being compared with the latter, and (*seek*) being taken out of the former and put to the latter, and (*wealth*) taken out or rather implied, in the former, the whole sentence is thus resolved, *Let no man seek his own wealth, but let every man seek another's wealth.*

And the word here translated *wealth,* is the same with that in *Rom. 13. 4,* and may not be taken only for riches, as Englishmen commonly understand it, but for all kinds of benefits, favors, comforts either for soul or body; and so here again, as before you must understand an Affirmative Commandment, as the Negative was before: and least any should say, If I may not seek my own good, I may do nothing; Yes saith *Paul,* I'll tell thee, thou shalt seek the good of another, whereas now all thy seeking helps but one, by this means thou shalt help many: and this is further enforced by these two circumstances, (no man) may seek his own, be he rich, learned, wise, &c. *But every man must seek the good of another.*

The point of instruction is taken from the very letter and phrase, viz.

Doct. 2. *A man* must *seek the good, the wealth, the profit of others.*

I say he *must* seek it; he must seek the comfort, profit and benefit of his neighbor, brother, associate, &c. His own good he need not seek, it will offer itself to him every hour; but the good of others must be sought, a man must not stay from doing good to others till he is sought unto, pulled and hauled, (as it were) like the unjust judge, for every benefit that is first craved, cometh too late. And thus the ancient patriarchs did practice, when the traveller and wayfaring men came by, they did not tarry till they came and asked relief and refreshment, but sat at the gates to watch for such, (*Judges 19. 20, 21*) and looked in the streets to find them, yea, set open their doors that they might freely and boldly enter in. And howsoever, some may think this too large a practice, since now the world is so full of people, yet I see not but the more people there is, the larger charity ought to be.

But be it so, as a man may neglect, in some sort the general world, yet those to whom he is bound, either in natural, civil, or religious bands, them he must seek how to do them good. A notable example you have in *David*, who, because there was twixt him and *Jonathan* a band and covenant, therefore he enquired, *Whether there was any left of the house of Saul, to whom he might shew mercy for Jonathan's sake*, 2 Sam. 9.1. So this people of *Corinth*, to whom *Paul* writeth, they were in a spiritual league and covenant in the *Gospel*, and so were a body. Now for one member in the body to seek himself, and neglect all others were, as if a man should clothe one arm or one leg of his body with gold and purple, and let all the rest of the members go naked. *1 Cor. 12. 27.*

Now brethren, I pray you, remember yourselves, and know, that you are not in a retired monastical course, but have given your names and promises one to another and covenanted here to cleave together in the service of God, and the King; What then must you do? May you live as retired hermits? and look after no body? Nay, you must seek still the wealth of one another; and enquire as *David*, how liveth such a man? How is he clad? How is he fed? He is my brother, my associate; we ventured our lives together here, and had a hard brunt of it and we are in league together. Is his labor harder than mine? surely I will ease him; hath he no bed to lie on? why, I have two, I'll lend him one; hath he no apparel? why, I have two suits, I'll give him one of them; eats he coarse fare, bread and water, and I have better, why, surely we will part stakes. He is as good a man as I, and we are bound each to other, so that his wants must be my wants, his sorrows my sorrows, his sickness my sickness, and his welfare my welfare, for I am as he is. And such a sweet sympathy were excellent, comfortable, yea, heavenly, and is the only maker and conserver of churches and commonwealths, and where this is wanting, ruin comes on quickly, as it did here in *Corinth*.

But besides these motives, there are other reasons to provoke us not only to do good one to another; but even to seek and search how to do it.

1. As first, to maintain modesty in all our associates, that of hungry wanters, they become not bold beggars and impudent cravers; for as one saith of women, that, when they have lost their shamefacedness, they have lost half their honesty, so may it be truly said of a man that when he hath lost his modesty, and puts on a begging face, he hath lost his majesty, and the image of that noble creature; and man should not beg and crave of man, but only of God. True it is, that as Christ was fain to crave water of the Samaritan woman, (*John 4. 5.*) so men are forced to ask sometimes rather than starve, but indeed in all societies it should be offered them. Men often complain of men's boldness in asking, but how cometh this to pass, but because the world have been so full of self-lovers as no man would offer their

money, meat, garments, though they saw men hungry, harborless, poor, and naked in the streets; and what is it that makes men brazen-faced, bold, brutish, tumultuous, but because they are pinched with want, and see others of their companions (which it may be have less deserved) to live in prosperity and pleasure?

2. It wonderfully encourageth men in their duties, when they see the burthen equally borne; but when some withdraw themselves and retire to their own particular ease, pleasure, or profit; what heart can men have to go on in their business? when men are come together to lift some weighty piece of timber or vessel; if one stand still and do not lift, shall not the rest be weakened and disheartened? Will not a few idle drones spoil the whole stock of laborious bees: so one idle-belly, one murmurer, one complainer, one self-lover will weaken and dishearten a whole colony. Great matters have been brought to pass where men have cheerfully as with one heart, hand, and shoulder, gone about it, both in wars, buildings, and plantations, but where every man seeks himself, all cometh to nothing.

3. The present necessity requireth it, as it did in the days of the *Jews*, returning from captivity, and as it was here in *Corinth*. The country is yet raw, the land untilled, the cities not builded, the cattle not settled, we are compassed about with a helpless and idle people, the natives of the country, which cannot in any comely or comfortable manner help themselves, much less us. We also have been very chargeable to many of our loving friends, which helped us hither, and now again supplied us, so that before we think of gathering riches, we must even in conscience think of requiting their charge, love and labor, and cursed be that

profit and gain which aimeth not at this. Besides, how many of our dear friends did here die at our first entrance, many of them no doubt for want of good lodging, shelter, and comfortable things, and many more may go after them quickly, if care be not taken. Is this then a time for men to begin to seek themselves? *Paul* saith, that men in the last days shall be lovers of themselves, (*2 Tim. 3. 2.*) but it is here yet but the first days, and (as it were) the dawning of this new world, it is now therefore no time for men to look to get riches, brave clothes, dainty fare, but to look to present necessities; it is now no time to pamper the flesh, live at ease, snatch, catch, scrape, and pill, and hoard up, but rather to open the doors, the chests, and vessels, and say, brother, neighbor, friend, what want ye, any thing that I have? make bold with it, it is yours to command, to do you good, to comfort and cherish you, and glad I am that I have it for you.

4. And even the example of God himself, whom we should follow in all things within our power and capacity, may teach us this lesson, for (with reverence to his Majesty be it spoken) he might have kept all grace, goodness, and glory to himself, but he hath communicated it to us, even as far as we are capable of it in this life, and will communicate his glory in all fulness with his elect in that life to come; even so his son Jesus Christ left his glory eclipsed for a time, and abased himself to a poor and distressed life in this world, that he might, by it, bring us to happiness in the world to come. If God then have delighted in thus doing good and relieving frail and miserable man, so far inferior to himself, what delight ought man to have to relieve and comfort man, which is equal to himself?

5. Even as we deal with others, ourselves and others shall be dealt withal. Carest thou not how others fare, how they toil, are grieved, sick, pinched, cold, harborless, so as thou be in health, livest at ease, warm in thy nest, farest well? The days will come when thou shalt labor and none shall pity thee, be poor and none relieve thee, be sick, and lie and die and none visit thee, yea, and thy children shall lie and starve in the streets, and none shall relieve them, for *it is the merciful that shall obtain mercy*; Mat. 5. 7. and *the memory of the just shall be blessed* even in his seed; *Prov. 10.* and a merciful and loving man when he dies, though he leave his children small and desolate, yet every one is mercifully stirred up for the father's sake to shew compassion, but the unkindness, currishness, and self-love of a father, is through God's just judgment recompensed upon the children with neglect and cruelty.

6. Lastly, That we may draw to an end; A merciless man, and a man without natural affection or love, is reckoned among such as are given over of God to a reprobate mind, (*Rom. 1. 30.*) and (as it were) transformed into a beast-like humor; for, what is man if he be not sociable, kind, affable, free-hearted, liberal; he is a beast in the shape of a man; or rather an infernal spirit, walking amongst men, which makes the world a hell what in him lieth; for, it is even a hell to live where there are such men: such the Scriptures calleth *Nabals*, which signifieth *fools*, (*Psal. 14. 1.*) and decayed men, which have lost both the sap of grace and nature; and such merciless men are called goats, and shall be set at Christ's left hand at the last day, (*Math. 25. 33.*) *Oh therefore seek the wealth one of another.*

Obj. But some will say, *It is true, and it were well if men would so do, but we see every man is so for himself, as that if I should not do so, I should do full ill, for if I have it not of my own, I may snap short sometimes, for I see no body showeth me any kindness, nor giveth me any thing; if I have gold or silver, that goeth for payment, and if I want it I may lie in the street, therefore I had best keep that I have, and not be so liberal as you would have me, except I saw others would be so towards me.*

Ans. This Objection seemeth but equal and reasonable, as did the Answer of *Nabal* to *David's* men, but it is most foolish and carnal, as his also was; for, if we should measure our courses by most men's practices, a man should never do any godly duty; for, do not the most, yea, almost all, go the broad way that leadeth to death and damnation, (*Luke. 13. 23, 24.*) Who then will follow a multitude? It is the word of God, and the examples of the best men that we must follow. And what if others will do nothing for thee, but are unkind and unmerciful to thee? Knowest thou not that they which will be the children of God must be kind to the unkind, loving to their enemies, and bless those that curse them? (*Mat. 5. 44, 47.*) If all men were kind to thee, it were but *publicans'* righteousness to be kind to them? If all men be evil, wilt thou be so too? When *David* cried out, *Help Lord, for not a godly man is left*, Psal. 12. 1. did he himself turn ungodly also? Nay, he was rather the more strict. So, if love and charity be departed out of this world, be thou one of them that shall first bring it in again.

And let this be the first rule, which I will with two others conclude for this time.

1. Never measure thy course by the most, but by the best, yea, and principally by God's word; Look not what others do to thee, but consider what thou art to do to them: seek to please God, not thyself. Did they in *Mat. 25. 44.* plead, that others did nothing for them? No such matter, no such plea will stand before God, his word is plain to the contrary, therefore, though all the world should neglect thee, disregard thee, and contemn thee, yet remember thou hast not to do with men, but with the highest God, and so thou must do thy duty to them notwithstanding.

2. And let there be no prodigal person to come forth and say, Give me the portion of lands and goods that appertaineth to me, and let me shift for myself; *Luke 15. 12.* It is yet too soon to put men to their shifts; *Israel* was seven years in *Canaan*, before the land was divided unto tribes, much longer before it was divided unto families; and why wouldst thou have thy particular portion, but because thou thinkest to live better than thy neighbor, and scornest to live so meanly as he? but who, I pray thee, brought this particularizing first into the world? Did not Satan, who was not content to keep that equal state with his fellows, but would set his throne above the stars? Did not he also entice man to despise his general felicity and happiness, and go try particular knowledge of good and evil; and nothing in this world doth more resemble heavenly happiness, than for men to live as one, being of one heart, and one soul; neither any thing more resembles hellish horror, then for every man to shift for himself; for if it be a good mind and practise, thus to affect particulars, *mine* and *thine*, then it should be best also for God to provide one heaven for thee, and another for thy neighbor.

Object. But some will say, *If all men will do their endeavors as I do I could be content with this generality,—but many are idle and slothful, and eat up others' labors, and therefore it is best to part, and then every man may do his pleasure.*

First, this, indeed, is the common plea of such as will endure no inconveniences, and so for the hardness of men's hearts, God and man doth often give way to that which is not best, nor perpetual, but indeed if we take this course to change ordinances and practices because of inconveniences, we shall have every day new laws.

Secondly, if others be idle and thou diligent, thy fellowship, provocation, and example, may well help to cure that malady in them, being together, but being asunder, shall they not be more idle, and shall not gentry and beggary be quickly the glorious ensigns of your commonwealth?

Thirdly, construe things in the best part, be not too hasty to say, men are idle and slothful, all men have not strength, skill, faculty, spirit, and courage to work alike; it is thy glory and credit, that thou canst do so well, and his shame and reproach, that can do no better; and are not these sufficient rewards to you both.

Fourthly, if any be idle apparently, you have a law and governors to execute the same, and to follow that rule of the Apostle, to keep back their bread, and let them not eat, go not therefore whispering, to charge men with idleness; but go to the governor and prove them idle; and thou shall see them have their deserts. *Acts 19. 38. 2 Thes. 3. 10. Deut. 19. 15.*

187

And as you are a body together, so hang not together by skins and gymocks, but labor to be jointed together and knit by flesh and sinews; away with envy at the good of others, and rejoice in his good, and sorrow for his evil. Let his joy be thy joy, and his sorrow thy sorrow: Let his sickness be thy sickness: his hunger thy hunger: his poverty thy poverty; and if you profess friendship, be friends in adversity; for then a friend is known and tried, and not before.

3. Lay away all thought of former things and forget them, and think upon the things that are; look not gapingly one upon other, pleading your goodness, your birth, your life you lived, your means you had and might have had; here you are by God's providence under difficulties; be thankful to God, it is no worse, and take it in good part that which is, and lift not up yourself because of former privileges; when *Job* was brought to the dung-hill, he sat down upon it, *Job 2. 8.* and when the Almighty had been bitter to *Naomi*, she would be called *Marah*; consider therefore what you are now, and whose you are; say not I could have lived thus, and thus; but say thus and thus I must live: for God and natural necessity requireth, if your difficulties be great, you had need to cleave the faster together, and comfort and cheer up one another, laboring to make each other's burden lighter; there is no grief so tedious as a churlish companion and nothing makes sorrows easy more than cheerful associates: bear ye therefore one another's burthen, and be not a burthen one to another; avoid all factions, frowardness, singularity and withdrawings, and cleave fast to the Lord, and one to another continually; so shall you be a notable precedent to these poor heathens, whose eyes are upon you, and who very brutishly and cruelly do daily eat and consume one another, through

their emulations, ways and contentions; be you therefore ashamed of it, and win them to peace both with yourselves, and one another, by your peaceable examples, which will preach louder to them, than if you could cry in their barbarous language; so also shall you be an encouragement to many of your christian friends in your native country, to come to you, when they hear of your peace, love and kindness that is amongst you: but above all, it shall go well with your souls, when that God of peace and unity shall come to visit you with death as he hath done many of your associates, you being found of him, not in murmurings, discontent and jars, but in brotherly love, and peace, may be translated from this wandering wilderness unto that joyful and heavenly Canaan.

AMEN.

See all of the Knowledge Keepers books on Amazon and at
KnowledgeKeepersBookstore.com!

Made in the USA
Las Vegas, NV
09 February 2025

17828275R00108